The Christian's Highest Good

Douglas Vickers

WIPF & STOCK · Eugene, Oregon

THE CHRISTIAN'S HIGHEST GOOD

Copyright © 2014 Douglas Vickers. All rights reserved. Except for brief quotations in critical publications or reviews, no part of this book may be reproduced in any manner without prior written permission from the publisher. Write: Permissions, Wipf and Stock Publishers, 199 W. 8th Ave., Suite 3, Eugene, OR 97401.

Wipf & Stock
An Imprint of Wipf and Stock Publishers
199 W. 8th Ave., Suite 3
Eugene, OR 97401

www.wipfandstock.com

ISBN 13: 978-1-62564-664-4

Manufactured in the U.S.A.

Scripture quotations are from the King James Version.

To the memory of
Miriam

Contents

	Preface	ix
one	The Issue Stated	1
two	The Identity and Offices of Christ	17
three	The Coming of Christ	39
four	The Christian's Highest Good	55
five	The Propitiation and Intercession of Christ	73
six	Christian Distinctives	87
seven	Mind, Heart, and Will	99
eight	Abiding in Christ	115
nine	The Christian's Prospect	131
	Bibliography	147

Preface

The principal proposition I address in this book is that the Christian's highest good consists in "fellowship with the Father and with his Son Jesus Christ," as the apostle John has stated that in the introduction to his first epistle. That fellowship follows from the redemptive work of Christ, and by reason of the renewing, regenerating work of the Holy Spirit of God in the soul an individual is admitted to the high privileges it conveys. By reason of its grounding in God the Father's adoption of the Christian believers as sons of God, that fellowship is, at its very inception, indissoluble. The Christian believer's *summum bonum*, his highest good, is to see God. That, in its ultimate sense, will accrue to the Christian in the day of our Lord's appearing, when the vision of God will be full in the face of Christ in his glorified human nature. But while in this life it is not possible to *see* God with the eyes of flesh, the Christian's highest good is to *know* God in fellowship with him.

The exposition of the meaning and implications of fellowship with God takes up a number of underlying and relevant issues. They have to do with both the *essential* and the *official* or *redemptive* identity of Christ, the extent of his propitiatory and intercessory work, and the manner in which those questions have been addressed in historic theology. Considered also are certain trends in thought which have influenced the changing patterns of the church's statement of its evangel. This has required notice of the assumption of the competence of unaided human reason and the anthropocentric orientation it has fostered, as that has infiltrated its influence into the church's statement of doctrine.

The book aims to clarify the practical and experiential significance of the fact that by God's salvific grace two classes of people exist: those who are in fellowship with God and are "walking in the light," to use the phrase from John's epistle, and those who still "walk in the darkness." The implications of that distinction are traced at some length in the context of an examination of the Christian character that is consistent with the privileged

Preface

state of fellowship with God. A final chapter considers the Christian's prospect that "when he [Christ] appears we shall be like him, for we shall see him as he is" (1 John 3:2).

As already indicated, in writing the following chapters I have been motivated and influenced by the text of the first epistle of John, though I have in no sense set out to provide a commentary on that highly important epistle. I acknowledge the influence of the valuable commentary on the first epistle of John by Robert S. Candlish, and as some aspects of my argument are dependent on it I make full acknowledgment of my indebtedness to it. Numerous commentaries on John's epistle are available, and I have acknowledged at some points of the book the helpful expository suggestions of Martyn Lloyd-Jones.

Parts of the first three chapters contain material that first found its way into a paper on "Why did Jesus Christ come into the world?" delivered at a meeting of the New England Reformed Fellowship (NERF) in September, 2013. I thank the Rev. David Green and the Executive Committee of NERF for their hospitality on that occasion. Parts of the remaining chapters are dependent on a syllabus on the first epistle of John that I prepared for the adult Sunday School of the West Springfield Covenant Community Church, Massachusetts, and I record my gratitude to the Rev. Al LaValley who facilitated that class.

As has been the case with a long list of books and professional papers I acknowledge with gratitude the skillful editorial assistance of Ann Hopkins. I retain full responsibility for the blemishes and infelicities that remain.

one

The Issue Stated

Nothing, in the context of cultural critique, impresses the mind more firmly than what is observable as the crippled search for meaning and authority. Criteria of knowledge, belief, and behavior are fractured. A half-millennium of comfortable confidence in the competence of human reason has dissipated. Its once assured modernity has transmuted into a postmodernism that is unsure of its direction, its internal coherence, and its capacity for the projection of truth. For the reality is that the ethos of the age has bogged us in a directionless individualism. There are no absolutes now, apart, perhaps, from the recognition of the trick that logic plays on us; the only absolute that has any currency and permits no denial is that there are no absolutes. That is the pointlessness of our time. What, therefore, it is urgent to ask, has the Christian church, or Christian men who have been called into the church, to say to the world at large? Is any meaning yet to be culled from the old pages of divine revelation, or are the claims that the church might once have made no longer accessible to recapture, recognition, or relevance?

We may ask a different question. What does it mean to be a Christian in our time? And how do the claims of Christianity stand against the contemporary complex of thought? Our answers will insist on the continued relevance of the classic Christian confession and will contemplate what our title has envisaged as the Christian's highest good. But in order to cast our discussion in adequate light it is necessary to reflect on two primary issues. First, what is to be said of the emergence in the history of thought of the virtually pervasive assumption of the competence and sovereignty of reason in the search for meaning; and how, if at all, has that influenced or infected the church's theology and doctrine? In other words, how has the elevation of the assumed competence of human reason and will diminished the biblical declaration of divine grace? Second, in what ways, as a result, have errant theologies advanced their claims and competed for attention and in doing so influenced the pulpit and troubled the pew?

Our objective in this chapter is to sketch briefly, first, some principal philosophic trends, and secondly their theological influence, that have brought us to our present malaise. We aim thereby to establish reference points against which the meaning of the Christian life and the place of the Christian in the world can be more readily established.

Reason and Autonomy

Philosophy has surrendered its search for answers to big questions, God is no longer a presupposition that orders investigative inquiry, and the smallness of our thought has sprung from the same assumption that Protagoras, the early Greek philosopher, advanced in his dictum that "Man is the measure of all things."[1] Alexander Pope, the eighteenth century poet, took up the strain in his philosophic poem, *Essay on Man*, where he concludes with the proposition: "Presume not God to scan; the proper study of mankind is man."[2] The absorption of thought with the preeminence of man, with the ultimate explanatory significance of man, had, of course, an earlier revival. At the beginning of what is generally referred to as modern philosophy, Descartes had shunted thought onto an anthropocentric track in the conclusion of his search for a "clear and distinct idea." He found that clarity in his awareness of his own identity and cognitive capacity. That, for him, was encapsulated in his familiar conclusion that "I think, therefore I am."[3] On the basis of that, and in "the innate knowledge of Descartes . . . based on

---

1. Protagoras's (480–410 BC) statement has been understood as "indicative of his relativism which ultimately rests upon his theory of perception according to which we know only what we perceive but not the *thing* perceived," Fishler, in Runes, *Dictionary of Philosophy*, 257. To that extent, Protagoras stands as an anticipator of the epistemological theory of Immanuel Kant to which we shall refer below, particularly the latter's claim that no knowledge of the *ding an sich*, the thing itself, is possible, that having been consigned by Kant to his so-called noumenal realm.

2. Pope, *Essay on Man*, 770.

3. Descartes, *Discourse on Method*. His "cogito, ergo sum," "I think, therefore I am," appears in Part IV of the *Discourse*.

the idea of the autonomy of man,"⁴ the assumption of the ultimate explanatory competence of man was firmly established. Van Til summed up the outcome in his observation that "the essence of the non-Christian position is that man is assumed to be ultimate or autonomous. Man is thought to be the final reference point in predication."⁵

In the seventeenth century, after the long medieval struggles and the seeming somnolence under ecclesiastical authority, after the partial release from the intellectual and cultural imperatives of the church that came with the Renaissance, and after the Reformation rediscovery of the sovereignty of God and the reality of the Creator-creature distinction, a remarkable twofold development occurred. On the one hand there was a consolidation in British and European thought of the systematic statement of biblical doctrine that the new breath of Christianity bequeathed; and on the other hand the century witnessed the birth, as has been said, of a new trend in an anthropocentric orientation of thought.

That latter trend reached definitive articulation in the philosophy of Immanuel Kant at the end of the so-called eighteenth-century Enlightenment, which advanced a new conception on the level of epistemology or the theories of knowledge or of what and how we know. In that, Kant stood definitively for the autonomy of man. Or to put it differently, he stood for the autonomy of theoretical thought. That followed from the way in which, combining elements of the rationalism that Descartes had fathered and the empiricism of Locke and the British philosophers that preceded him, he reached the conclusion that the individual was autonomous and sovereign in the search for knowledge. That was because what was knowable was not, as Kant understood it, objective reality as such (Kant's *ding an sich*), but the perceptions of that reality as they were interpretable by certain "categories" existent in the individual human mind. In effect, that is, each individual knower constructed his or her own reality by the manner in which those individual categories of mind brought their interpretative influence to bear on external objects of knowledge. The categories inherent in the human mind, then, impress meaning on external reality.⁶ Leaving aside Kant's

---

4. Van Til, *Defense of the Faith*, 172. Van Til later referred to his own system of thought as set "over against the man-centered view of men like Plato, Aristotle, Descartes, Locke, Leibnitz, Kant, etc.," in Geehan, *Jerusalem and Athens*, 125.

5. Van Til, *Christian Theory of Knowledge*, 12–13.

6. Among numerous discussions of Kant's epistemological theory see Windelband, *History*, 537–50.

more detailed argument, it had then become imperative philosophic dicta that man was autonomous and sovereign in knowledge. In essence, that was the meaning of what Kant advanced as his "Copernican revolution" in the theory of knowledge.

It became all too true that so far as assumedly cultured thought was concerned, "all roads lead to Kant." The shadow of Kant has been cast very long and has had determinative influence on theological thought ever since and up to the present day. It is true that at the so-called beginning of modern theology at the hands of Schleiermacher in the early nineteenth century, an attempt was made to rebel against the intellectual strictures of the Kantian system of thought. But Schleiermacher simply proposed the autonomy and sovereignty of man in a different guise. For him, Christian theology was properly characterized by a new subjectivism, thereby again orienting its thought on the assumed autonomy of man, in the development of what became referred to as man's feeling of absolute dependence on God.[7] At that time, consistent with the impulse to thought that the new subjectivism bequeathed, the grand objectivities of the Christian revelation, the being and will and purposes of God, the reality of human sin, and the categories of redemption by the coming into the world of the Second Person of the Godhead in the Person of Jesus Christ, were submerged. Again the individual person was sovereign and autonomous.

But because the escape from Kant was ineffective and abortive, Kantian conclusions have been determinative in Christian thought in a further damaging respect. For Kant, as we have observed, what was knowable in the world of fact was what it was, or what it became, by reason of the interpretation of it by the sovereignty of the human mind, by the so-called categories of mind. But that was not all that was implied. For Kant, the only objects of knowledge were what was observable, or more particularly the impressions or perceptions of what was observable, in the actual world of empirical fact. That world, Kant denominated the "phenomenal realm," and only what existed in the phenomenal realm was, in the sense that has been indicated, knowable. Objects of knowledge were confined to the empirical

---

7. Schleiermacher, *The Christian Faith*, 19. See the evaluation of Schleiermacher's theology in Mackintosh, *Types of Modern Theology*, 60–100. Mackintosh concludes that "Schleiermacher's failure to take Revelation seriously . . . gives rise to the natural accusation that for him theology is less concerned with God than with man's consciousness of God. The shadow of what is known as 'psychologism' lies over all his work," ibid., 94, and "[Schleiermacher] put discovery in place of revelation, the religious consciousness in the place of the Word of God, and the 'not yet' of imperfection in the place of sin," ibid., 100.

realm. Beyond the phenomena thus observable, things and entities as they were in themselves (the *ding an sich*) were beyond the reach of knowledge. Only the impressions that they generated were knowable. But further, beyond Kant's phenomenal realm there existed what he referred to as the "noumenal realm" in which objects may exist but were not in themselves knowable.

In that important connection, it is sufficient for our present purposes to observe that for Kant, God was consigned to the noumenal realm and was therefore unknowable. God may exist. Or he may not. Kant insisted that no adequate proof of the existence of God could be stated, and he somewhat gallantly concluded that while, then, it could not be definitively stated that God existed, by the same token it could not be definitively stated that he did not exist. There was no way to know. For Kant, God was not an element of the knowable, or a subject of what he called "pure reason," but an assumption of "practical reason."[8] Kant said that he "abolished knowledge to make room for faith."[9] But his "faith," of course, had no correspondence at all with the faith that the sovereign grace of God imparts to an individual and which stands, as a result, as the instrumental cause of salvation.[10] We shall return to the point.

It is not necessary for our present purposes to follow all the ways in which the assumption of human autonomy and the elevation to primary determinative status of the introspective individual worked out their effects in the nineteenth and twentieth centuries. We observe that in doing so they further infected Christian theology. Nineteenth-century positivism, early twentieth-century existentialism, the negativism in thought that gave birth to the later "God is dead" theology that revived the thought of the nineteenth-century philosopher Nietzsche, and the now somewhat aborted

---

8. In his *Critique of Practical Reason*, 109, Kant stated that "It is morally necessary to assume the existence of God.... This moral necessity is *subjective*... and not *objective*." That followed from his earlier *Critique of Pure Reason*, 306–7, where Kant had concluded that "These remarks will have made it evident... that the ideal of the Supreme Being, far from being an enouncement of the existence of a being in itself necessary, is nothing more than a *regulative principle* of reason.... It exists merely in my own mind, as the formal condition of thought, but not as a material and hypostatic condition of existence."

9. Greene refers to "Kant's sharp distinction between knowledge and faith" in "The Historical Context and Religious Significance of Kant's *Religion*" in "Introduction" to Kant, *Religion*, lxxv.

10. Van Til observes: "Kant made room for 'faith' but not for biblical faith," *Christian Theory of Knowledge*, 58.

postmodernism, all exerted their influences.[11] But above it all, the upshot of the on-going influence of the Kantian consolidation of the postulate of human autonomy remained. The result was that the fact and the doctrine of the being and sovereignty of God, the revealed attributes and character of God, the declared salvific purposes of his will, and the true standing of man before and in the sight of God, have been substantially evacuated from theological thought.

The Christian, Christianity, and the Church

Our objective in the chapters that follow is to examine at some length two principal questions, the answers to which throw light on the identity and status of the Christian person, the status and meaning of Christianity in the present social and intellectual complex, and the state, responsibility, current health, and prospects of the church. First, bringing into focus the coming into this world of the Second Person of the Godhead to become Jesus Christ, what is to be understood as the reasons for his coming, taking up in that question the revealed identity of the Lord Jesus Christ himself? And second, what, in the light of that, is to be understood as the privileges that accrue to the Christian person who, by the sovereign grace of God, is called into the body of the church of which Jesus Christ is the head?

Reason exists to believe, it must be confessed at the outset, that the Christian mind, particularly as it reflects on the deposit of truth that has come down from the Reformation rediscovery and rearticulation of biblical doctrine, holds the relevant truths only uncertainly at this time. The Christian church is seemingly unaware of its true identity, and its message and witness to the world is, as a result, muted and indistinct. What, in short, has the church to say to the world and to its decaying twenty-first-century culture? Who speaks for the church, and how does, or should, the church speak to the issues of morality that appear at this time in clear confusion? Is

---

11. The reference to the work of Nietzsche is of interest on several counts. McLean observes on Nietzsche's reaction to the eighteenth-century so-called Enlightenment: "Nietzsche critiqued the use of human rationality as the sole measure by which truth is validated. . . . Rationality has, de facto, taken the place of the concept of 'God' as the ultimate foundation of truth. This substitution of human rationality for God is what Nietzsche's madman meant by his famous announcement of the 'death of God.': 'Whither is God?' he cried; 'I will tell you. *We have killed him*—you and I. All of us are his murderers'," *Biblical Interpretation*, 64. See Nietzsche, "The Gay Science," in *The Portable Nietzsche*, 95.

there, in fact, any clear demarcating line between the culture of the church and the culture of the world? Does the church possess a cogent or coherent evangel to announce? And as it follows from such questions, what is to be said of the place of the Christian individual in both the church and the world? And what are the privileges and prospects before him?

It would be a gross and unconscionable mistake, of course, to suggest or conclude that the evangel that the church has historically held in true biblical proportion nowhere comes to expression at the present time. Quite to the contrary, instances of Reformed-evangelical Christianity in true biblical character are readily identifiable. Institutions of sound Reformed theological education have come into existence and continue to bear biblical witness. Heavy volumes of biblical exposition and helpful treatises on theological loci and the progressive Christian life have appeared, to the undoubted benefit of the church and the Christian believer. The republication of highly valuable works from older times has added weight to the confession of the church and the culture of Christian confessors. Valuable monographs on aspects of Christian doctrine have appeared.

Our task at present is in no sense to diminish the considerable value of the considerable good that exists for the searching in the contemporary church, its agencies, and its centers of scholarship. But therein lies the problem that motivates our present concern. In too many instances, there is reason to conclude, the influence of the philosophico-intellectual issues and forces we have already identified have appeared to tarnish both the scholarship and the witness of the church. Our task in what follows is not that of providing an extensive critique of the sources and influences of theological problems that have infected the well-being and doctrines of the church. We write in a much more modest vein. But at the risk of incompleteness and insufficient clarification, some of the more prominent deleterious preoccupations of recent Christian theology can be identified.

What is to be said, for example, of the sovereignty, the purposes, and the knowledge of God, and, as a result, of the divine participation in human affairs? What, after all, does God know, and how, if at all, is that knowledge relevant to human history and development? The recently fashionable theology of the so-called Open Theism addresses the question. That system of thought, advanced, no doubt, in sincerity by Christian theologians, denies the omniscience of God in a singularly dangerous respect. In brief, the Open Theism argues that of course God is omniscient. But the meaning imported to omniscience is not that of historic Christianity. It is contained in the statement that God is omniscient in the restrictive sense that he knows all that is available to be known. The significance of that proviso, as it is understood by the Open Theism theology, is that the future has not yet eventuated and is not therefore available to be known, and God, therefore, does not know the future. It is not necessary to argue at length the respects in which such a theology has destroyed the very godness of God, in that it constitutes a flat denial of God's sovereign will and purpose, his omniscience and omnipotent power by which, as the letter to the Ephesians has it, he "worketh all things after the counsel of his own will" (Eph 1:11).[12]

To the contrary, a Christian theology that is grounded in God's self-revelation and in the biblical data that conveys the revelation of his will and purpose holds securely to the eternal necessity of God, meaning that he is in his being not dependent on any cause external to himself, and to the sovereignty of his own will. There is no entity, event, or possibility external to the Godhead on which, or in relation to which, God is, or could have been, dependent. If the contrary were true, God would not be the God of the Scriptures. He would be, in one sense or another, a god made in the image of man's imagination.

Other thought systems that, in one way or another, have twisted and corrupted the biblical truths on which the Church's theology has been historically founded have also infected the witness of the church. In more recent times a so-called New Perspective on Paul has argued for a reconstruction of the entire covenantal theology that the church has historically held. The New Perspective argues that the historically received traditions of Pauline theology have misunderstood and misrepresented what the apostle had set out to say. It has proposed a radically different view of the covenantal theology that has traditionally been derived from the Pauline writings. The essential argument proceeds in the following terms. By God's grace, it is said, a certain people, Israel of old, were assumed to be members of God's saving covenant, though the grounds on which that assumption came to effect are not clearly stated. But the upshot of the New Perspective system is that once having been assumed into the covenant, individuals maintained their status and remained within the covenant by their observance of, and adherence to, certain so-called identity or boundary markers and their obedience to what they interpreted as the law and commandments of God.

---

12. For expansive evaluations of the Open theism theology see R. K. Wright, *No Place for Sovereignty* and Frame, *No Other God*. See also the valuable reference to Open Theism and a reference to the work of Frame in Oliphint, *God With Us*, 11–12.

Those boundary markers included, for the Jews, circumcision, certain food laws, and Sabbath-keeping. Beyond that, it is argued that the apostle Paul's problem was that of convincing the Jews that the Gentiles should be admitted to the kingdom without subscription to, and obedience to, those Jewish identity or boundary markers. That, of course, is a far cry from what is to be understood as the Pauline doctrine of justification and its place in the larger conspectus of covenantal theology. We shall return to that in due course.

But other aspects of the New Perspective theology deserve brief notice. It was claimed, for example, that the righteousness of God was to be understood as God's faithfulness to his covenantal promises. N. T. Wright claims that "For a reader of the Septuagint . . . 'the righteousness of God' would have one obvious meaning: God's own faithfulness to his promises, to the covenant."[13] The faithfulness of God in that respect is, of course, beyond doubt. But when, in the New Perspective's construction of the meaning and significance of the covenant, such an interpretation is carried over as the sole meaning relevant to Paul's theology, it avoids and misrepresents completely the meaning of God's righteousness as portrayed in the Pauline vocabulary and doctrine. At the most elemental level, and beyond addressing what is to be regarded as God's essential righteousness or the righteousness implicit in the conformity of all of his actions to the dictates of his own essential holiness, the righteousness of God rests in the conveyance of his righteousness to the repentant sinner who comes to him in saving faith. The sinner is thereby made the beneficiary of the imputation to him of the substitutionary forensic righteousness of Christ. The fatal flaw, the rejection of the fact and doctrine of imputation, is clear in Wright's following argument: "If we use the language of the law court, it makes no sense whatever to say that the judge imputes, imparts, bequeaths, conveys or otherwise transfers his righteousness to either the plaintiff or the defendant. Righteousness is not an object, a substance or a gas which can be passed across the courtroom. . . . To imagine the defendant somehow receiving the judge's righteousness is simply a category mistake. That is not the way language works."[14]

---

13. N. T. Wright, *What Saint Paul Really Said.* 96.

14. Ibid., 98. For a critical evaluation of recent debates on the doctrine of justification, including a survey of doctrinal development and a response to the arguments of Wright and others, see Dunson, "Do Bible Words have Bible Meaning?" 239–60.

The Christian's Highest Good

The New Perspective on Paul is a revival of old heresies that are calculated to betray the entire doctrine of the church as that addresses the justification of man in the sight of God. Adequate literature on the highly important controversies that arose from the New Perspective on Paul is readily available.[15] Our intention at this point is simply to illustrate that in that errant theological system the biblical theology of the church has again been brought under attack, and to the extent that well-meaning theologians are captured by it, the witness of the church has in recent times been diminished.

The doctrine of the church has been further brought under attack in recent times by the emergence of a so-called Federal Vision theology. A principal issue in this thought system, and a point at which its divergence from historic Christianity is prominent, has to do again with an erroneous interpretation of the meaning of the salvific covenant between God and man. It is sufficient for our present purposes to confine comment to one essential point from among many that are discussed in the literature referred to below. It has to do with what is to be understood as the significance of the church's sacrament of baptism and its relation to the meaning of God's covenant.

By the administration of the sacrament of baptism, it is claimed by the Federal Vision theology, one is admitted to covenant membership in the fullest sense and one is thereby joined in union to Christ. Now the high doctrine of the Christian believer's union with Christ is to be carefully guarded, and that union conveys to the Christian the highest privilege that admission to the kingdom of God implies. It provides the foundation, the entry point, to the fellowship with the Father of which the apostle John, for example, speaks at great length in his first epistle. But it is precisely at that point that the Federal Vision theology has had a seriously corrupting influence.

A prominent proponent, Rich Lusk, crystallizes the issue in his summary statement that "In baptism we are brought covenantally and publicly out of union with Adam and into union with Christ. When this occurs, one is 'born again,' not in the sense we have come to speak of regeneration . . . but in the covenantal sense of being brought out of Adam's family into God's family. . . . In this relationship, one has, in principle, all the blessings in the heavenly places delivered over to him as he is 'in Christ.'"[16] That

---

15. See Waters, *Justification* and Eveson, *The Great Exchange*, 110–57.
16. Lusk, "Do I Believe in Baptismal Regeneration?" cited in Waters, *Federal Vision*, 226–27. See also ibid., 359.

formulation, and the confusion regarding the covenant that it carries with it, might appear to be rescued by the words "not in the sense we have come to speak of regeneration." But what Lusk has done is to point up the very difficulties of the Federal Vision theology at that point. For on the one hand the Federal Vision theology argues that by baptism one is joined to Christ in the fullest sense and meaning of that privilege, and at the same time it is said that one may subsequently fall away from and surrender the benefits and privileges that were previously enjoyed. Lusk himself goes on to make the point. He says that "these blessings [are] considered from the standpoint of the covenant rather than the eternal decree, [and] are mutable."[17] But what is thereby proposed is that what is "mutable" are, in fact, the highest benefits that baptism at first conferred, namely nothing less than union with Christ. The theological problem thereby brought to the surface is the attempt to draw a distinction between, as Lusk has stated it, the grace of regeneration on the one hand and the reality of union with Christ within the terms of the covenant of grace on the other. For union with Christ, in the full sense that the Federal Vision theology in one breath claims, and "all the blessings in the heavenly places delivered over to him as he is 'in Christ'" are, as the Scriptures present it, precisely what is conferred by the conveyance to an individual of the Holy Spirit's grace of regeneration.

More extensive reference to Federal Vision texts confirms that in similar ways baptism is understood to confer on the one who is the subject of the ordinance the highest reality of union with Christ. But at the same time, the Federal Vision theology envisages one's possible apostasy from that high position. Douglas Wilson, for example, expands the confusion when he raises the question of what he refers to as "reprobate" individuals who have received the benefits of baptism: "Baptism is covenantally efficacious. It brings every person baptized into an objective and living covenant relationship with Christ, whether the baptized person is elect or reprobate. Baptism is always to be taken by the one baptized as a sign and seal of his ingrafting into Christ. If the person is reprobate, he will be cut out of the vine . . ."[18] The doctrinal problem in Wilson's argument is highly significant. It is recognizable on two levels. First, that highly questionable teaching claims that the "seal" implicit in baptism has been understood to have been conveyed to the reprobate person. Second, when, at a later time, the reprobate person has been "cut out of the vine," it is from that high

17. Ibid., 227.
18. Cited in Waters, *Federal Vision*, 209–10.

status of having been "sealed" into "living relationship with Christ," sealed not merely into a notional relationship but, as Wilson claims, a "living" relationship, that the "cutting out of the vine" occurs.[19]

Errant theologies beyond those to which we have drawn attention trouble the church and call in question the integrity of its evangel. It is argued by some that Christian subscription automatically, but in respects that cannot be clearly defined, endows the believer with material prosperity. The spirituality of the kingdom of Christ is diminished, and the world with its persuasions and predilections is invited into the church and given, it would seem, gaping accommodation. In newly emerging churches new fashions of thought and worship are more readily identifiable with contemporary postmodern culture than with the historic gospel.[20] In short, in more instances and in more ecclesiastical communions than need to be identified at length, the reduction of the biblical gospel is due to the fact that the view of Christ and his redemptive accomplishment is too low because the view of man is too high.

There is substantial reason to conclude that the new theologies being proposed to the church would take it far outside the limits of its classic and historic confessional standards. In doing so, those theologies are aimed to puncture the church's confessional reliance on the biblical revelation on which its stance has hitherto been based. It is therefore extremely difficult to understand the manner in which certain confessionally Reformed churches have at the present time permitted to remain within their credentialed communities those whose professed alliance is with one or the other of the errant theologies we have briefly noted.

A Preliminary Summing Up

The preceding discussion has established two reference points whose significance will throw their light on what follows. First, it becomes clear from even a less than complete survey of the history of opinion that the assumption of the autonomy of man, the assumption of the explanatory

---

19. For a full discussion see Waters, *Federal Vision*, and for an introduction to some origins of the Federal Vision theology see Shepherd, *The Call of Grace*.

20. The literature on the Emergent Church and its theological reconstructions is now extensive. Minimum reference might be made to McLaren, *A New Kind of Christianity* and the same author's *A New Kind of Christian*, and Carson, *Becoming Conversant with the Emerging Church*.

competence of unaided human reason, has been accorded determining status in the explanation of affairs and conditions in the world. And further, that assumption of autonomy has affected and infected the theology of the church. Second, the struggle for the preservation of the church's theology is not only set against the thought forms and pressures of the world in the respects just implied, but also against tendencies to errant doctrinal formulation within the church itself. The negative influence of the assumption of human autonomy and the impact, as a result, on the church's theology can be illustrated in a respect in which the testimony of the church has been severely tarnished in the present time.

Consider, for the moment, the respect in which that assumption of human autonomy, or, again, the postulate of the primacy of the human intellect, has come to expression in the doctrines of the church. Reflect, that is, on the competence of the mind as it exists in the human state characterized by the post-Adamic and fallen condition. An important debate directed to precisely that condition occurred in the fourth century between the great Augustine and a Celtic monk named Pelagius. The outcome of the Augustinian-Pelagian controversy determined important aspects of subsequent orthodox theological doctrine relating to sin and salvation. Pelagius, in short, argued that Adam's fall did not convey to his posterity any disability in the faculties of soul, and that after the fall men were in precisely the same state as to their competence of will as they had enjoyed in their initial created state. The will was free to turn to God or not to turn to God at any time, it was claimed. It was the duty of man to obey God, and he was both obliged and free to do so. He should obey God, and if he chose to do so he could.

The Roman Catholic doctrine took up and consolidated the essence of the Pelagian scheme. But it can be said to be "Semi-Pelagian" in the following respect. Pelagius had said, in effect, that as to the faculties of soul, man in his postlapsarian state was perfectly healthy. The medieval theology that followed him said, to the contrary, not that man was completely healthy but that he was sick and in need of assistance. Man, that is, needed the assistance of the grace of God in his move towards repentance and faith, but he was well enough to cooperate with divine grace as it was made available to him. Grace, that is, was congruent with man's own effort and merit. The Reformers, to the complete contrary, argued not that man was sick and in need of the help of the grace of God, but that, as the Scriptures declare, as to his faculties of soul and his competence to know God he was dead; he was "dead in trespasses and sins" (Eph 2:1). His renewal unto life was therefore due completely and sovereignly to the unmerited grace of God.

It is worthy of note that the debate between Pelagius and Augustine, where the latter stood for the biblical orthodoxy, was repeated in the sixteenth century in a corresponding argument between Calvin, the great systematizing theologian and exegete of the Reformation, and a Roman Catholic scholar named Albert Pighius. It was repeated again at the Synod of Dort in the early seventeenth century when the Remonstrant theology of Arminius and his followers, which had arisen in a semi-Pelagian form, was rejected.[21] On the level of evangelism it recurred again in the eighteenth century when the Reformed theology of George Whitefield was set against the semi-Pelagianism of John Wesley and the Methodist movement he founded. And it is unfortunately true that semi-Pelagianism has been formative of much of the theology of the present-day evangelical church.

The matter of the sovereignty of the grace of God in salvation can be put in other terms. Salvation, we may say, is not an *autosoterism*, nor a *synergism*, but to the glory of the grace of God it is a *divine monergism*. We define the terms briefly as follows. "Autosoterism" means essentially "self-salvation," or salvation that is achieved by one's completely unaided efforts, by one's own design and implementation. It means that in one way or another man saves himself. If one were to hold to the pure Pelagian theory and if, therefore, he insisted that he needed no outside help at all towards salvation, he would be claiming the complete efficiency and effectiveness of a system of autosoterism. "Synergism," on the other hand, means that a cooperation of some form of outside help is necessary to salvation. Semi-Pelagianism, with its notion of congruent grace, is a form of synergism. To the extent that the present-day evangelical church holds to forms of cooperation between man and God in salvation, it propagates some form or other of synergism. That most usually comes to expression in contemporary evangelicalism through its insistence, against biblical argument to the contrary, on the freedom of human will. The relevant doctrinal issues will be discussed more fully in the following chapters.

Some theologians and commentators who have held to the necessity of the grace of God in the movement of the soul to salvation have in several ways, and in semi-Pelagian form, oriented their argument on the concept

---

21. For a valuable discussion of Arminianism and its defects and the contrary doctrines of God's electing and saving grace, see Packer's "Introductory Essay" in Owen, *The Death of Death*, 1–25.

of the cooperation of man with divine grace. The following example will illustrate the kinds of difficulties involved in such doctrinal formation. There has occurred an "emphasis upon both the initiating power of God's grace and the need for willing cooperation with it."[22] As to the efficiency of the human will in its fallen state, it is said that while "our own wills [do not] contribute anything towards the attainment of eternal life . . . they have a kind of negative veto which can obstruct the work of salvation."[23] The concept of that negative veto is to be recognized carefully. For it is said in such theologies that "our only capacity for making a contribution to our spiritual renewal is the capacity to say yes or no to what is divinely initiated."[24] There is a "malaise of the fallen human condition" for which there is "no non-Christian remedy."[25] But it appears, in the semi-Pelagian schemes we are currently noting, that the best to be said about the human contribution to righting the condition of things is that "disciplines have to be imposed on the appetites and desires" leading the individual astray, such that the grace of God is inhibited from intervening in the soul in a manner necessary to salvation.[26] In something of an apparent contradiction, the author whose conclusion we have just referred to also observes that "Whatever else being saved may involve, it can never possibly put you in the position of being able to tell God his business."[27] But the damage has already been done. For the previously claimed ability of the will to say yes or no to the grace of God has already "told God his business."

All such theological inventions as these deny in one way or another the sovereignty and the irresistibility of the grace of God. If, however, it is held, consistently with the expansive testimony of the Scriptures, that salvation is by the grace of God alone, then it is held that salvation is a divine monergism. "Monergism" means that only one efficient cause is operative in, and solely capable of bringing to effect, the objective of salvation. The doctrine of salvation that came down to us from the theology of the Reformation is unambiguously monergistic. The argument as to why that is so will be seen to lie at the heart of the scriptural statement of the status

---

22. Blamires, *Recovering the Christian Mind*, 77–78.
23. Ibid., 78.
24. Idem.
25. Ibid., 83.
26. Ibid., 78.
27. Ibid., 89.

of man in his fallen and sinful state and the remedy in the substitutionary work of Christ that God has addressed to it.

The Way Ahead

The testimony of the church to the world at large rests essentially in the gospel of salvation. That gospel states that in the predeterminate council of the Godhead before the foundation of the world a Covenant of Redemption was formed, the substance of which was that redemptive offices were assumed by the respective Persons of the Godhead. The Second Person of the Godhead would come into the world to become Jesus Christ, taking a true human nature in body and soul, with all the faculties of human soul, into union with his divine nature. In that human nature he would, by his sinless life and substitutionary death, redeem those whom the Father had given to him for that purpose. The Holy Spirit undertook to call to Christ and apply to those for whom Christ died the gifts and benefits he purchased for them, to complete within them the sanctification to which they were designed by eternal decree, and to conduct them to glory. To bring to full effect the designs and objectives of that Covenant of Redemption a Covenant of Grace that guaranteed the fulfillment of God's promise of redemption was formed and instituted, the parties to which were God on the one hand and his chosen people as represented by Christ on the other. The more expansive meaning and implications of the gospel of God's grace will engage us in the chapters that follow. The essence of what remains to be addressed has to do with the ways in which, in the providence of God, the terms of his eternal decrees have been worked out in historic fact. That calls for a discussion of the consequent relations between God and man, having regard to the true status and competence or otherwise of man, and the realization and full expression of the benefits that Christian salvation implies and involves.

In short, if the biblical integrity of the gospel is to be preserved and maintained in the witness of the church, the critical questions that demand answer are "Who, in fact, was Jesus Christ?" and "Why did Jesus Christ come into the world?" Then if those who are the beneficiaries of the redemptive acts of Christ are in fact joined in union to him, what are the highest blessings and privileges that union carries with it?

We turn immediately in the following chapter to the first of those questions.

two

The Identity and Offices of Christ

The gospel of the grace of God in the redemption of sinners emanates from the council of the Godhead before the foundation of the world. Its design is grounded in the redemptive offices of the Persons of the Godhead as declared in the eternal Covenant of Redemption. That covenant implies that no more ultimate explanation of the course of human affairs exists than that of the sovereign will and decree of God, executed in his works of creation, providence, and redemption. And no more ultimate explanation spans human history than that of which the coming and the redemptive accomplishment of Christ is the watershed. At the turning point of the history of the church the apostle Peter stated to the incredulous crowd that it was "by the determinate counsel and foreknowledge of God" that the remarkable events they had witnessed had occurred (Acts 2:23). And when the newly assembled people of God raised their prayer for the disciples, Peter and John, who had been falsely arrested, they acknowledged that the authorities in their malevolence had done "whatsoever thy hand and thy counsel determined before to be done" (Acts 4:28). At the heart of the gospel stands the declaration that God "worketh all things after the counsel of his own will" (Eph 1:11).

But the covenantal structure of Christian thought and the sovereignty of God in salvation have been substantially betrayed in our time. While that is so, it is true, of course, that a serious and prominent examination of historic covenantal theology has been maintained in the context of Reformed theological witness. Among the most recent offerings, K. Scott Oliphint's *Covenantal Apologetics* has set out to make a significant advance on the level of apologetic witness.[1] Theologians Bryan D. Estelle, F. V. Fesko, and David VanDrunen have forced a new examination of the respects in which the Mosaic covenant, while it is to be understood as a form of administration of the covenant of grace, exhibits a works principle and, indeed, has been referred to by a long line of Reformed theologians as partaking of elements of the covenant of works.[2] But in the contemporary evangelical-theological context, the church's doctrinal formation finds its determinative nexus too often in its focus on man and his supposed capacities, intellectual and ethical, to the neglect of the biblical explanation of his fallen condition. For that reason, the objective realities of God's implementation of his covenantal purposes in the salvation of the elect people he gave to his Son to redeem (John 17:6, 9) have not found a ready place or served as the orientation of thought. The biblical data that state that we are all the fallen children of Adam are only lightly handled. While the imputation to us of the guilt of Adam's sin extends its disastrous deposit to the fact that we come into the world with a fallen nature, that fact does not find a ready place in the most common evangelical expressions.

Any purported explanation of the human condition that sets out to avoid the reality of our original sin sits oddly with the biblical data and historic confessional theology. The Westminster Shorter Catechism states the case: "The fall brought mankind into an estate of sin and misery," and "The sinfulness of that estate whereinto man fell consists in the guilt of Adam's first sin, the want of original righteousness, and the corruption of his whole nature, which is commonly called original sin, together with all actual transgressions which proceed from it."[3] An adequate explanation of the human condition is discoverable only in a theology that understands that God, in setting forth his remedy for sin, has "delivered us from the power of darkness, and hath translated us into the kingdom of his dear Son" (Col 1:13). The Christian has been moved by the grace of God from his condition of solidarity in Adam to a new solidarity in Christ (Rom

---

1. Oliphint, *Covenantal Apologetics*. The apologetic move by Oliphint leaves room for dissent and discussion among Reformed scholars, but it is to be commended for its address to some important questions in the practice of apologetics.

2. Estelle, Fesko, and VanDrunen, *The Law is not of Faith*. The treatment of a highly important question to which that book is addressed, namely whether the Mosaic covenant is to be understood as a "republication" of the covenant of works, has attracted dissent among Reformed theologians, but it presents a challenging review of theological commentary on its subject.

3. Westminster Shorter Catechism, Questions 17–18.

5:12–21). That is the outcome of the triune God's execution of his eternal decree of redemption.

What was observed in the preceding chapter as the widening influence, in the history of thought in general and in the doctrines of the church, of the postulate of the competence of human reason in the discovery and formulation of truth has born its fruit in a contemporary man-centered, or anthropocentric, theology. Schleiermacher, whom we observed as the founder of modern theology in the early nineteenth century, has fathered a distant offspring. But Christian thought, to the extent that it is biblically responsive, is to be Christocentric. In that, it is theocentric. Its determining nexus and orientation is what has been revealed as the being, will, and purpose of God. For God has set forth Christ, "in whom are hid all the treasures of wisdom and knowledge" (Col 2:3).

Why, then, it is to be asked, did Jesus Christ come into the world? Theological doctrine that is grounded in divine revelation permits and requires various responses to the question. We shall return to that question more fully in the following chapter. But at this point we observe that beneath a biblically sustainable answer lies the identity of Jesus Christ, both his *essential* identity and his *official*, or *economic*, or *redemptive* identity. When we refer to the *essential* identity of Christ we have in view his distinguishable identity within the triune Godhead. "There are three persons in the Godhead," the Catechism states, "the Father, the Son, and the Holy Ghost; and these three are one God, the same in substance, equal in power and glory."[4] It is not being said there that the essence of the Godhead is, in some sense that would remain to be defined, distributed among the divine Persons. It is being stated that the full essence of God resides fully in each of the Persons. The divine mind, the divine affections, and the divine will are wholly in each of the Persons. It follows that Jesus Christ, who came into the world to be the Savior of sinners in accordance with the determinate divine decrees was none other than the Second Person of the eternal Godhead. When he was in this world, a divine Person who took a full human nature into union with his divine nature, he did not divest himself of his eternal glory or of the full attributes of his divine Personhood; though he laid aside the signs or insignia of that glory.[5] It follows, moreover, that when he was

---

4. Ibid., Question 6.

5. The so-called kenotic theory that reads the text at Philippians 2:8 as saying that Christ did, in fact, lay aside his eternal glory when he was in this world is a complete misreading of the text.

The Christian's Highest Good

in this world, as to his divine nature our Lord was both in this world and in heaven with the Father and the Holy Spirit, while in his human nature he was in this world (John 3:13).[6] Now, as to his divine nature he is both in heaven and in this world, while as to his human nature he is in heaven.

The meaning of the descriptive term *economic* in reference to Christ's redemptive identity refers in theological usage to the distribution of redemptive offices among the Persons of the Godhead. In short, it was the redemptive office of the Father to elect a certain, defined, and unalterable number of people to eternal salvation and to give them to his Son to redeem. It was the redemptive office of the Son to come into the world, to take a sinless human nature into union with his divine nature, to satisfy in that human nature all of the demands of the righteous law of God on behalf of the people the Father gave to him, and having done that, to bear in his death the penalty due to them for their sin. It was the redemptive office of the Holy Spirit to call to Christ those for whom he died, to convey to them the gifts and benefits that Christ purchased for them, to sanctify them, and to conduct them to glory. We speak, therefore, of the *official* identity of Christ, intending thereby reference to the redemptive office that he came into the world to discharge.

As to his *essential identity*, Christ came, he said, to declare God to us: "No man hath seen God at any time; the only begotten Son, which is in the bosom of the Father, he hath declared him" (John 1:18). "I am in the Father, and the Father in me" (John 14:11), he said on a memorable occasion (declaring the perichoresis or circumincession of the Godhead),[7] when he replied to Philip: "He that hath seen me hath seen the Father" (John 14:9).

---

6. See the comment on John 3:13 in Hendriksen, *John*, 500–501.

7. The perichoresis of the Godhead refers to the indwelling in one another of the divine Persons. That highly important theological datum has been misunderstood and misrepresented by Keller in his *Reason for God*, 222–36, notably 224, where he refers to "The Dance of God." Keller states that "The life of the Trinity is characterized not by self-centeredness but by mutually self-giving love.... That creates a dynamic, pulsating dance of joy and love." Keller concludes from his notion of the "dance of God" that "each [Person of the Trinity] voluntarily circles and orbits around the others," cited in Bidwell in the following reference, 114. Keller, contrary to a clear understanding of the term, falsely understands that "dance" of the Persons of the Trinity as explaining the divine perichoresis. See the response by Bidwell in Campbell and Schweitzer, *Engaging with Keller*, 97–133. Among other grounds of dissent, Bidwell properly observes that Keller's "Dance of God" "does not uphold the unity of the Godhead based on essence ... does not promote a balanced presentation of the trinity as found in the Nicene Creed ... has the danger of tritheism ... [and] undermines the authority structure that is directly related to redemption."

The Identity and Offices of Christ

"The Jews took up stones to stone him" when he made his definitive existential claim, "I and my Father are one" (John 10:30–31). But the essential identity of Christ is rendered indistinct, if not completely lost, in forms of modern theology, such as that of Paul Tillich, to note an extreme example. Tillich concluded that God is to be "understood first of all as being-itself or as the ground of being."[8] It is, of course, appropriate to say, with Herman Bavinck, for example, that "God makes himself known as absolute being."[9] Bavinck continues: "He [God] makes himself known as the one who *is* in an absolute sense.... God is exclusively from himself, not in the sense of being self-caused but being from eternity to eternity who he is, being not becoming."[10] But modern theology in the fashion of Tillich, in its argument that "The being of God is being itself.... or the ground of being," concludes that "If God is *a* being, he is subject to the categories of finitude, especially to space and substance,"[11] and therefore, "It is as atheistic to *affirm* the existence of God as it is to *deny* it. God is being-itself, not *a* being."[12] It follows from such doctrinal propositions that the autotheotic nature of the Second and Third Persons of the Godhead, and the distinguishable properties of God the Son and God the Holy Spirit, are not brought into the relief that the Scriptures and historic Reformed theology have ascribed to them.[13] The *essential identity* of the *Person* of Jesus Christ is not, thereby, well preserved.

Our principal interest in the present work is in the biblical data regarding the *redemptive* office of Christ, who, as has been said, came into the world as the Second Person of the eternal Godhead to *become* Jesus Christ for our redemption. But as we shall see more fully, that redemptive office

---

8. Tillich, *Systematic Theology*, 235. Tillich argues that God is not "*a* person," and asserts that he is only "the ground of everything personal and carries within himself the ontological power of personality," ibid., 245. Frame rejoins that for Tillich, God is an "impersonal principle." See Frame, *Systematic Theology*, 38. For an argument contrary to that of Frame and also Cornelius Van Til (Van Til, *Systematic Theology*, 229) on the question whether God is to be said to be "*a* person," and on the possibility of confusing "person" and "essence" in relation to God, see Horton, *The Christian Faith*, 285. See also the rejoinder by Frame in op. cit., 487–88. Warfield, of Princeton Theological Seminary in the late nineteenth century, observed that "The great thing to be taught the ancient people of God was that the God of all the earth is one person," *Biblical Doctrines*, 127.

9. Bavinck, *Reformed Dogmatics*, 152.

10. Idem.

11. Tillich, op. cit., 235.

12. Ibid., 237, italics partially added.

13. See Tillich's conclusion that "Trinitarian monotheism is not a matter of the number three. It is a qualitative and not a quantitative characterization of God," ibid., 228.

derives its significance from the eternal identity of God the Son whom the Father *sent* into the world. The apostle Paul, focusing his thought on the official or *redemptive identity* of Christ, makes the summary claim to Timothy that "Christ Jesus came into the world to save sinners" (1 Tim 1:15). The Lord himself said that he came to "lay down [his] life for the sheep" (John 10:15), for those whom, before the foundation of the world the Father had given to him to redeem (John 17:6). But before we look more directly at the import of what has just been said, we reflect on some common perceptions, in historic and literary opinion, of the identity of Jesus Christ.

Who Is Jesus Christ?

For two thousand years men have wrestled with the questions: "Who is Jesus Christ?" and "How are we to explain the presence of Jesus Christ in this world?"[14] It would be a mistake, of course, to imagine that those questions have been universally engaged or have agitated the minds of all men at all times. The realities of the human state as it naturally exists as a result of Adam's fall argue eloquently to the contrary. But to reflective minds the questions of the identity and the objectives in life of Jesus Christ have been, in one way or another and at various times, imperative.

Among cultivated minds the question of "Who is Jesus Christ?" has spawned an extensive literature, both before and since Albert Schweitzer's classic work, originally published in 1906 under the title *The Quest for the Historical Jesus*.[15] The inquiry continued through the heyday of neo-orthodoxy and Rudolph Bultmann's so-called demythologization of the Scriptures, where the pre-existence, virgin birth, crucifixion, and resurrection of Jesus were under heavy attack.[16] For the common man, the slumber of sin and his subjection to Satan have substantially quieted the quest. The "strong man armed keepeth his palace and his goods [captives in the slumber of sin] are in peace" (Luke 11:21). "There is no fear of God before their eyes" (Rom 3:18). That is true, even though there are in every person "intimations of immortality," to use the poet Wordsworth's phrase, a *sensus deitatis*, a sense of God that is suppressed when it rises unbidden to the level of

---

14. See Vickers, *Being and Belief*, 4.

15. See also McLean, op. cit., 62, for "diverse and contradictory portraits of the historical Jesus" in the work of recent scholars. For an earlier review see Strimple, *The Modern Search for the Real Jesus*.

16. See Bultmann, *Jesus Christ and Mythology*.

consciousness (Rom 1:18). There is a memory in the race of men. There exists a memory of paradise that rises unrecalled to the mind. By virtue of man's creation as the image of God, there is finally irrepressible in the soul the awareness of God and the *semen religionis*, the seed of religion, that constitutes man as essentially a religious being. For that reason man will necessarily and naturally worship some one or the other God. Either he will hold to a godly religion, in obedience to the true God of the Scriptures who has revealed himself, or he will worship a god made in his own image. He will, if he turns his back on the true God, become an idolater and he will fall to the level of the recalcitrant Israelites of old in their embrace of spiritual adultery.

But the questions persist, and the Holy Spirit disturbs the mind at his sovereign command. The church from earliest times struggled to settle its conviction on the very same points. The early heresies regarding the Person of Jesus Christ, and the ecumenical councils of the church that addressed them and reached a firm christological settlement, warrant careful attention. The issues under debate had to do essentially with what was to be understood in relation to the being of the divine Godhead, and in that context focus fell pointedly on the question of the identity of the Second Person of the Godhead, God the Son. Four principal controversies and four councils of the church deserve recognition and will be noted briefly, though they cannot detain us at length at this time.

Controversies and Councils

A clear and sustainable response to the question, "Why did Jesus Christ come into the world," makes it necessary to proceed with some care on two fronts. First, as we have anticipated, we must consider the doctrinal basis of what is to be held regarding the divine personhood of Jesus Christ; and second, it is necessary to encapsulate in biblical terms the meaning and significance of his coming.

It has unfortunately to be said that confessing evangelicalism has historically, and notably at the present time, varied in its responses to the questions we have raised and it does not present a uniform confession in its statement of the evangel. For what was accomplished, it has to be asked, by the life and by the death of the man Jesus Christ who appeared among men for their eternal benefit? Is unique significance and efficacy to be attributed to his life as well as to his death? What, then, were the benefits that accrue to those for whom Christ lived and died, if, in fact, the extent of the efficacy that his life and death projected can be specified? If the apostolic deliverance in 1 Corinthians 1:30 is to be relied on as definitive, in what respect does the fact that Jesus Christ is our *sanctification* as well as our *righteousness* convey meaning to the way in which our questions are answered? In short, and quite apart from a fuller expansion of their biblical grounding, what are we to say of the place that must finally be occupied in our confession by the arguments to which we drew attention in the preceding chapter of such luminaries as Augustine versus Pelagius, Calvin versus Pighius, the Synod of Dort versus Arminius, the Amyraldians and their attempts at theological-doctrinal mediation, Whitefield versus Wesley, and their contemporary Reformed and evangelical offspring among whom the historical controversies find re-expression?

Considerations of personhood are necessarily prior to those of office and function. Being is prior to act and behavior. It is for that reason that the early church was at pains to settle the question of the identity and Person of Jesus Christ before, on the basis of its settlement on that level, it could proceed with its fuller confessional articulation. The heresy of Arianism, for example, argued that the Person of Jesus Christ did not possess a true and full divine nature. He existed before his birth in this world, it was claimed, but not from eternity. He was a creature of God, but he was not eternally divine. "Arius admitted that the Son was produced before all other beings, and held that He was God's agent or instrument in the creation of them all."[17] But he did not exist in eternal consubstantiality with the Father. The heresy of Arianism was rejected by the church at the Council of Nicea in the year 325, and in the following years the worthy Athanasius argued strongly in support of what had then been agreed as the orthodox position on the doctrine of the Person of Christ.

But further debates on the question followed. Sabellius, a presbyter of the church in the third century, taught that what the orthodox church held to be the Second and Third Persons of the divine Trinity were, in fact, only two different powers of the one God, emanating from the divine essence.[18] Other heretical doctrines troubled the church. Eutychianism argued that two natures did not exist as distinct natures in Christ, but that at the incarnation the human nature was absorbed into the divine. The result was that Christ existed as one person with one nature. An opposite error was

17. Cunningham, *Historical Theology*, 1:282. See also Shedd, *History*, 1:392–408.
18. See Cunningham, op. cit., 267–306. See also Shedd, op. cit., 1:253–61.

The Identity and Offices of Christ

held by the Nestorians who held that the two natures, divine and human, existed in Jesus Christ as what were, in effect, two separate persons.[19] The debates continued at the Councils of Constantinople in 381 and Ephesus in 435, and a definitive conclusion on the doctrine of the Person of Christ was reached at the Council of Chalcedon in 451.[20]

At that time it was resolved that the two natures were united in the Person of Christ "without confusion, without change, without division, and without separation."[21] The first two of those defining characteristics state that there was no communication of properties from the one nature to the other. The divine nature remained divine, and the human nature remained human. Neither nature took on the properties of the other. At the incarnation there was no commingling of the eternal (divine) and the temporal (human). At the incarnation the Second Person of the Godhead took into union with his divine nature a created, finite, and temporal human nature. He now lives in the heavens in his divine and human natures, not having divested himself of his humanity at his resurrection and ascension. In his divine and human natures he ever lives to make intercession for those who are the subjects of the redemption he accomplished. In the context of the doctrine of the being and essence of God as it is held by the Christian confession, God the Son and God the Holy Spirit are fully and eternally God in their own right. The Second and Third Persons of the divine Trinity, that is, are autotheotic. The full essence of the Godhead resides in each of the three distinguishable Persons of the Trinity. The realities of the eternal generation of the Son by the Father, and the eternal procession of the Holy Spirit from the Father and the Son are well-established elements of the orthodox Christian confession.[22]

Consider, against that background, what is to be said of the coming into the world of Jesus Christ. "God so loved the world that he *sent* his only begotten Son" (John 3:16). And "God loved us and *sent* his Son to be the propitiation for our sins" (1 John 4:10). He was not always and from eternity Jesus Christ. He came into the world to *become* Jesus Christ for our redemption. It is therefore necessary at that point to recognize the twofold

---

19. See the discussion of "Principal Heresies in Christology" in Shedd, op. cit., 1:392–98.

20. On Eutychianism, Nestorianism, and the Chalcedonian Settlement, see Cunningham, op. cit., 307–20.

21. See Van Til, *Defense of the Faith*, 32.

22. A fuller discussion of these important doctrines is contained in the appendix, "because Jesus was not yet glorified," in Vickers, *Discovering the Christian Mind*, 149–78.

mystery of his incarnation. Two divine miracles were involved. First, it was said to the virgin that "The Holy Ghost shall come upon thee, and the power of the highest shall overshadow thee" (Luke 1:35), intimating that as the human womb was prepared for the reception of divine impregnation the entailment of sin was broken, and the child to be born was without sin.[23] The second miracle was the Holy Spirit's act of impregnation of the sanctified egg of the mother and the consequent emergence of a created, finite, and temporal human nature. God the Holy Spirit did not create a fetus for implantation in the womb of the virgin. For Christ, as to his human nature, was born of the *substance* of the mother. If that had not been so, he could not have been truly human and thereby an acceptable and effective substitute for sinners. That necessity and fact indicate, first, that the divine Person who came into the world did, in fact, possess a full human nature, with all the faculties of soul and body that characterize humanity, yet without sin. And second, the actual impregnation of the egg of the virgin, that was necessary to establish true human nature, actually occurred.

The human nature that our Lord possessed, therefore, is to be understood and recognized as a created, finite, and temporal human nature. It was created, but only by impregnation; it was finite in that it was truly human and not divine; it was limited to the capacities of humanness in its scope and function, except, as we shall see, as it was supported in its human experience and act by the Holy Spirit; and it was temporal in an important respect. The deity of our Lord was, of course, atemporal, meaning that God exists in full essence outside of time, and that time itself is a created entity, created as a mode of finite existence. So, therefore, given what has been declared as the oneness and unity of the Persons of the Godhead, the *divine nature* of Christ is characterized by atemporality. But the *human nature* in view in the Person of Christ is, in its restriction to true human finitude, bound to the temporal character of finite existence.

But it is to be carefully guarded, as the Chalcedonian settlement implies, that the man Jesus Christ was not, as a result, a human person. The misstatement of the evangelical confession that Jesus was a human person must be scrupulously avoided. Jesus Christ was not a human person. As Berkhof has judiciously put it in his discussion of "The Unipersonality of Christ," "The Logos assumed a human nature *that was not personalized,*

---

23. Matthew Henry, the Puritan commentator, observes on the "overshadow thee" in Luke 1:35 that "She shall conceive by *the power of the Holy Ghost*, whose proper work and office is to *sanctify*, and therefore to sanctify the virgin for this purpose." *Exposition*, 585.

that did not exist by itself."[24] The divine Second Person of the Godhead, in voluntary condescension as agreed in the predeterminate council of the Godhead, took into union with his divine nature a human nature with all the properties of humanness, "in true body and reasonable soul."[25] Jesus Christ, the divine Son of God, that is, possessed the full faculties of human soul, intellect, affections, and will. And it was that human soul that, on the cross, he committed to the Father in his statement: "Into thy hands I commend my spirit" (Luke 23:46). It follows as an important point of christological confession, that in the Person of Christ there were two minds, a divine and a human, two capacities for affection, a divine and a human, and both a divine and a human will. When we ask who it was that walked the dusty roads of Galilee, who healed the sick and raised the dead and opened the eyes of the blind, we say that it was the eternal Son of God in human nature. Charles Wesley grasped the reality clearly in his well-known verse: "Veiled in flesh the Godhead see; hail the incarnate Deity."[26]

The late nineteenth-century Reformed theologian at Union Theological Seminary, W. G. T. Shedd, observed in that connection: "When these two natures are *united* in one theanthropic person, as they are in the incarnation, the divine determines and controls the human, not the human the divine."[27] Shedd had previously stated that "it is the divine nature, not the human nature, which is the base of Christ's person."[28] Further, "the divine nature constantly supports the human nature under all the temptations to sin that are presented to it. . . . It deserts the humanity so that it may suffer for the atonement of sin, but it never deserts the humanity so that it may fall into sin itself."[29] We shall return to the important matter of the presence and function of the Holy Spirit in the act of atonement that Christ performed on the cross. But it can be said in anticipation at this point that as it was in his human nature, not his divine nature, that Christ passed through eternal death on our behalf, in his doing so he was supported by the Holy Spirit.

The humanity and the divinity of Christ are declared by our Lord himself in his statement to Mary Magdalene immediately following his

---

24. Berkhof, *Systematic Theology*, 312–22, italics added. See also Schaff, *Creeds*, 1:29–34.

25. Westminster Shorter Catechism, Questions 21–22.

26. Charles Wesley, "Hark! The Herald Angels Sing." In *Trinity Hymnal*, 203.

27. Shedd, *Dogmatic Theology*, 2:332.

28. Ibid., 269.

29. Ibid., 335.

resurrection: "Go to my brethren, and say unto them, I ascend unto *my Father*, and your Father; and to *my God*, and your God" (John 20:17, italics added). In his commentary on Paul's second epistle to the Corinthians, Charles Hodge observes that "Jesus Christ is a designation of the . . . historical person . . . to whom God stood in the relation at once of *God* and *Father*. Our Lord had a dependent [human] nature to which God stood in the relation of God, and a divine nature to which He stood in the relation of Father."[30] As to our Lord's relation to the Father in his divine nature, the focus of Hodge's well-taken point is on the fact that the relation between the Father and the Son is unique, and is uniquely different from that between the Father and the Holy Spirit. The Spirit is not the Son of the Father. The Spirit and the Son exist in distinguishable Personhood.

The confusion on these highly important points in the evangelical and even in the purportedly Reformed literature might be instanced by a single reference to the work of Robert Peterson. In the first edition of his *Calvin's Doctrine of the Atonement* Peterson observed properly that "*God* Became a *Man* for our Salvation."[31] But in his second edition, published under the title *Calvin and the Atonement*," that reference was changed to read "*God* became a *Human Being* for our Salvation."[32] But it is to be held to the contrary that Jesus Christ was not a *human* being, or a *human* person. He was a *divine* being. Jesus Christ, as the pericope in Philippians 2:6–8 eloquently asserts, was God and man, fully man in all human faculties and in imputed covenantal responsibilities. But he was not a human person.

The question we have raised, therefore, is to be understood as referable to twofold levels: first, the *eternal Son of God* came into the world for the reasons and purposes that have been indicated; and second, the *human nature* that he assumed came into the world by the Holy Spirit's miraculous act of impregnation. Jesus Christ was therefore without sin, so that by his being made "perfect through suffering" (Heb 2:10) he was qualified to offer himself as the substitute for sinners in the discharge of his priestly office on the cross. As to the matter of his qualification, Philip Edgcumbe Hughes has summarized the issue in his valuable commentary by saying: "It is fitting that our Redeemer should have been *made perfect through suffering*:

30. Hodge, *Commentary*, 653, italics added. I am indebted for this reference to Hughes, *Paul's Second Epistle to the Corinthians*, 10. We say regarding our Lord, the second Person of the Godhead, that as to his *nature* he is autotheotic, while as to his *Person* he is of the Father. See Berkhof, *Systematic Theology*, 94.

31. Peterson, *Calvin's Doctrine of the Atonement*, 11, 21, italics partially added.

32. Peterson, *Calvin and the Atonement*, 25.

first, because his completely victorious suffering of temptation of every kind (Heb 4:15) was essential to his achievement of that perfection which *qualified* him to offer himself on the cross as the spotless Lamb of God in the place of sinners (1 Pet 1:18f.; 3:18); second, because his suffering and death at Calvary annulled the power of Satan and set free the 'many sons' who were destined for glory; and third, because his own experience of *human suffering* in the body he assumed has enabled him, as a compassionate high priest to aid and strengthen at all times those who are afflicted with trials and temptations."[33]

The Priestly Office of Christ

The redemptive office of Christ expands its meaning to exhibit Christ as our prophet, priest, and king. Those offices, as they are clearly observable in the Old Testament record, are understandable as anticipations of the status and office that Christ would occupy in God's redemptive plan. He came as the antitype of the types that had pointed to him. He came as the second Adam (1 Cor 15:45, 47) of which our first parent, Adam, was "the figure [type] of him that was to come" (Rom 5:14). And similarly, the high priest under the earlier form of administration of God's covenant of grace, and the prophets in their office of communicating the will of God to the people, were types of Christ. The prophets represented God to the people; and the priests represented the people to God.[34] Those two important representations are combined in the Person and work of Christ.[35]

Christ, the greater son of David, fulfills the office of king of which David was the type and anticipator. In that earlier administration of God's covenant, Israel was both the nation and the church, "the church in the wilderness" (Acts 7:38). The church in that age, designated by God "a kingdom of priests," was a "holy nation" (Exod 19:6), and now, since God's redemptive purpose has been fulfilled in the coming of Christ, the church is in itself the "holy nation" (1 Pet 2:9) of which Christ is the head. And in his kingship over the church, which is now distinct from the nations of the world, he is the antitype of those earlier kings. He has inherited the throne of David, as it was said of old that "the Lord God shall give unto him the

---

33. Hughes, *Hebrews*, 100, italics of "qualified" and "human suffering" added.
34. See the very valuable discussion in Young, *My Servants the Prophets*, 28.
35. See Westminster Shorter Catechism, Questions 24–26.

throne of his father David" (Luke 1:32). The promise that God had given to Nathan the prophet regarding David was now realized: "I will establish the throne of his kingdom for ever . . . and thine house and thy kingdom shall be established for ever before thee; thy throne shall be established for ever" (2 Sam 7:13–16). When Christ came, the promise was fulfilled: "But unto the Son he saith, Thy throne, O God, is for ever and ever" (Heb 1:8).

Regarding the priestly office of Christ the catechism states that "Christ executes the office of a priest, in his once offering up of himself a sacrifice to satisfy divine justice, and reconcile us to God, and in making continual intercession for us."[36] Two aspects of his discharge of that office are immediately important. First, Christ, as the antitype of the priests of old, was, in his offering "to satisfy divine justice," both the offering and the priest who made the offering. He was himself "the lamb of God which taketh away the sin of the world" (John 1:29). "The blood of goats and calves" could not definitively take away sin, "but by his own blood he [Christ] entered once into the holy place, having obtained eternal redemption for us" (Heb 9:12). "Ye were not redeemed with corruptible things . . . but with the precious blood of Christ . . . who verily was foreordained before the foundation of the world, but was manifest in these last times" (1 Pet 1:18–20).

The substitutionary aspect of the death of Christ in dealing with sin is explained in terms of the imputation of guilt and righteousness that was involved. We encountered the concept and doctrine of imputation at an earlier stage, when we observed that it is a serious fault of the doctrines promulgated by the New Perspective on Paul that, as Wright in particular clearly stated, to speak of the imputation that we now have in view as in no sense tenable.[37] But the issue calls for careful attention and is a vital part of the transactions between the Father and the Son in the accomplishment of redemption.

The nub of the issue is that in his substitutionary atonement the guilt of the sins of the people for whom he died was imputed to him, or, that is, was placed to his account. The sinless Son of God died in his human nature for those whom the Father had given to him for that purpose. Sin had entered the world in human nature, and a sacrifice for the payment of the penalty of sin must be made in human nature. But how could that be done? Man himself could not pay the penalty for his sin. In all the capacities of his soul he was estranged from God and enslaved to Satan and sin, "dead

36. Ibid., Question 25.
37. See chapter 1, n.14.

The Identity and Offices of Christ

in trespasses and sin" (Eph 2:1). Any man could only, therefore, unless the grace of God intervened, pay the penalty for his own sin in the eternal perdition that sin against a holy God warranted. Before man himself could have any standing before God the grace of God that creates new life within an individual by the regenerating work of the Holy Spirit must first endow the soul with the gifts of saving faith and repentance. And then, with that newness of life can the sinner turn to Christ. But if, because of the disabilities under which he exists by nature, man himself is unable to pay the price of his own redemption, how could redemption ensue? At that point the issue of imputation enters.

When our first parent, Adam, fell by repudiating his covenantal obligations to God, the guilt of his sin was imputed to, or in the reckoning of God placed to the account of, all those who would descend from him by ordinary generation.[38] That imputation was an immediate imputation. The word "immediate" in that statement of doctrine does not refer to immediacy in time; though the imputation did, of course, occur at the point in time immediately on Adam's sin. But "immediate" in our present context refers to the fact that there was no mediating cause or entity on the grounds of which the imputation in the accounting of God took place. The imputation of sin, that is, was *immediate* and not *mediate*.[39] The imputation was grounded only in the eternal will of God, entirely apart from any intramundane or temporal cause.

At the death of Christ, there occurred similarly what we may refer to as a reciprocal immediate imputation. The guilt of the sin of the people for whom Christ died was imputed to Christ, and the righteousness of Christ was imputed to them. When we refer to the righteousness of Christ in that context we do not have in view his *essential* righteousness that inheres in him by reason of his identity as the Second Person of the Godhead; or, that is, his righteousness as God by which we mean that all the actions, designs, purposes, and decrees of God are consistent with the essential and inherent holiness that he possesses in his eternal being. When we say that it is not Christ's essential righteousness that is imputed to the repentant sinner, it is meant that the individual does not, for that reason, partake of the essence of the Godhead. There is no such thing, that is, as the divinization of man. The righteousness of Christ that is placed to the sinner's account is a *forensic* righteousness; that is, the righteousness that comes from the

---

38. Westminster Shorter Catechism, Question 16.
39. See the highly valuable discussion in Murray, *Imputation*, 42–70.

perfect fulfillment of the demands of God's law and commandments. The term "forensic" has to do with the situation that exists in relation to, and because of, law. Christ impeccably fulfilled the demands of the law of God. In that, he was forensically righteous. By reason that the forensic righteousness of Christ is thus imputed to the sinner who comes to Christ in faith and repentance, God looks on that individual as though he had himself fulfilled the demands of the law, and as though he himself had paid the penalty for his having broken the law. Such is the immeasurable extent of God's grace and mercy that he has set forth in his Son.

By that reciprocal imputation the individual who has thus come to Christ has entered a state of justification before God. He was once *ungodly*, in that he had broken the law of God; "Christ died for the ungodly" (Rom 5:6); now he is regarded in the counsels of heaven as *godly*, for all the demands of the law have been met on his behalf. In that great exchange, God's declarative, forensic statement of justification has set the individual free from the law of sin, condemnation, and death, and has transferred him to the state of righteousness, justification and life.[40] A definitive transference has taken place. But the ground of the sinner's status that has thus been so remarkably changed is that Christ, by the imputation of the sinner's guilt to him, has been *constituted* guilty. And by reason of that constitution, God the Father could truthfully *declare* his Son guilty and lay upon him the punishment of sin. And similarly, by the corresponding act of imputation the sinner has been *constituted* righteous, so that God could truthfully *declare* him righteous. Such are the remarkable terms in which justification before God has been established.

In God the Father's act of constituting his Son guilty, Christ was thereby "made sin for us" (2 Cor 5:21). The Son of God was made sin, in that he was made guilty, not guilty of his own sin, but of the sin of those for whom he died. And being thus constituted guilty, the death that Christ died was his final act of active obedience to the law of God. For the law said that the guilty one must die. What a remarkable exchange the grace and mercy of God accomplished in that eternally meaningful act. But it is to be carefully observed also that in that divine act of imputation, while Christ was made to be sin, while our sin was laid upon him, he was not made or constituted a sinner.[41] If he were held in that sacred moment to have been constituted

---

40. See Murray, *Romans*, 202.

41. Horton has misleadingly observed that "Jesus Christ, sinless in himself, becomes the greatest sinner who ever lived," *The Christian Faith*, 621. See in the following footnote

The Identity and Offices of Christ

a sinner, the meaning of the entire redemptive act on the cross would be vacated. For the substitution that was involved in Christ's act of redemption was meaningful only because our sin was laid on him who was completely without sin. It was the sinless Son of God, the Second Person of the eternal Godhead who made the atonement for sin. But further, it was in his human nature in which he died for us that he was sinless.

The possibility of misunderstanding, at this important point, of the imputation involved in the substitutionary death of Christ has been addressed in particularly clear terms in a classic commentary that is worthy of extended statement: "God, declares Paul, made the Sinless One sin for us. It is important to notice that he does not say that God made Him a *sinner*; for to conceive of Christ as sinful, or made a sinner, would be to overthrow the very foundation of redemption, which demands the death of an altogether Sinless One in the place of sinful mankind. But God made him *sin*; that is to say that God the Father made His innocent incarnate Son the object of His wrath and judgment, for our sakes, with the result that in Christ on the cross the sin of the world is judged and taken away. In this truth resides the whole logic of reconciliation."[42]

The meaning in its full extent is ineffable, in that any words that we can command by reason of the language capacity we have in our human finitude cannot possibly compass the meaning of what was involved. Christ died in his human nature. He could not die in divine nature. Indeed, his death in human nature was precisely necessary to accomplish eternal salvation for those who had sinned in human nature. But it was "the Lord of glory" (1 Cor 2:8) who was crucified, and ineffable though it is, it was the

---

the danger of a possible misreading of Calvin's comment on the point.

42. Hughes, *Corinthians*, 213. In his commentary on 2 Corinthians 5:21 John Calvin asks: "How are we righteous in the sight of God?" and his answer follows: "It is assuredly in the same respect in which Christ was a sinner," *Corinthians*, 2:242. Calvin is not saying there that Christ was made or constituted a sinner. While Christ was not *made* a sinner, as Hughes has judiciously observed, he was, as Calvin goes on to say, "dealt with *as* a sinner." As the guilt of sin that Christ bore was not that of any *essential* or *intrinsic* sin of his own, "not for his own offenses," as Calvin observes, so, as Calvin's paragraph clearly states, the righteousness that we consequently possess is not Christ's *essential* righteousness conveyed to us, but is a forensic righteousness imputed to us as the forensic righteousness of Christ. Hodge, following Calvin, similarly observes that Christ "who was without sin was treated *as* a sinner," in the sense that, vicariously, "he suffered the punishment of death." Hodge, *Systematic Theology*, 2:510. The point of Calvin's comparison is that as the imputation of Christ's forensic righteousness to us does not make us holy, so the imputation of our guilt to Christ does not make him a sinner. Our holiness derives not from our justification but from our regeneration.

Person of our Lord who died for us in his human nature. And the *Person* of our Lord was, throughout his life and in his death, impeccably sinless.

In the transaction between the Father and the Son when Christ bore our sin on the cross, when he was made to be sin for us, the Father did not look on him as being in his own person a sinner. Mystery though it is, and ineffable the meaning in its ultimate divine relation, the eternal love between the Father and the Son was not, and could not, be broken, not even in the cry of dereliction from the cross, "My God, why hast thou forsaken me?" (Matt 27:46). The Father loved the Son even as he poured out his wrath against him, against the guilt of sin that he bore. The very godness of the Godhead, the eternal indwelling of the Son, with the Holy Spirit, in the Father, speaks its witness. Oh eternal love! That God himself, in the Person of his Son, should die for us who rebelled against him and his covenantal faithfulness. In the very death of the cross, God the Father looked upon the Son whom he loved and was satisfied that in his impeccable innocence the Son, in the perfect righteousness that he had sustained in his human nature, allowed the guilt of his people's sin to be laid upon him. Therein he bore the Father's wrath and saved the host that God, in his eternal jealousy and design, has elected to share his glory with him. The smile of the Father would soon return, and in his temporal death Christ the redeemer would give his human soul again to the Father. He would soon return to the heavens as the victorious high priest and intercessor for his people, glorified again, as he had prayed: "And now, O Father, glorify thou me with thine own self with the glory that I had with thee before the world was" (John 17:5).

Let us observe the meaning of the substitutionary death of Christ in summary terms. When he paid the penalty for sin on the cross, was Christ guilty? Yes he was guilty, not of his own sin, for he was sinless, but of the sin of those for whom he died. He was guilty because our sin was placed to his account. Our guilt was laid upon him. "The LORD hath *laid on him* the iniquity of us all" (Isa 53:6). Did the Father then regard his Son as in his intrinsic personhood a sinner? No, because as a *person* he was not intrinsically guilty, for he was the eternally pure, sinless Second Person of the Godhead and, further, in his human nature that he had assumed he was perfectly sinless. The guilt that was laid on Christ was true and punishable guilt, but so far as the *Person* who bore the guilt was concerned, it was not an *intrinsic* guilt. It did not belong to him personally. It was an *extrinsic* guilt.

When we look at the substitution of Christ for the sinners he redeemed, at the exchange of guilt and righteousness involved in the divine transaction that consummated our Lord's redemptive accomplishment, we see something of the wonder of the grace of God toward us. On the important and vitally relevant fact of the believer's constitutive righteousness and justification, John Murray has written insightfully: "Justification is both a declarative and a constitutive act of God's free grace. It is constitutive in order that it may be truly declarative. God must constitute the new relationship as well as declare it to be. The constitutive act consists in the imputation to us of the obedience and righteousness of Christ."[43] Acknowledging that the truthfulness and righteousness of God are involved at that point, Turretin has stated in that connection: "God cannot show favor to, nor justify anyone without a perfect righteousness. For since the judgment of God is according to truth, he cannot pronounce anyone just who is not really just. . . . By the righteousness and obedience of one, Christ, we are constituted righteous. . . . Justification takes place on account of the suretyship of Christ and the payment made for us by him."[44]

A second aspect of Christ's discharge of his priestly office warrants further reflection. The statement of the Catechism has emphasized that in his priestly office Christ has "reconciled us to God." The high import of that reconciliation will engage us at length in the following chapters. By reason of that redemptive accomplishment, the Christian believer becomes the beneficiary of the highest blessing that God accords to those whom Christ redeemed, nothing less than "fellowship with the Father" (1 John 1:3). The apostle Paul crystallized what is involved: "Through him [Christ] we both have access by one Spirit unto the Father" (Eph 2:18). Before we observe in the following chapters further aspects of what was involved, we underline at this stage the remarkable fact that in his Person and in his priestly office Christ brings us, his people, into the very throne room of the Father.

We reflect on a further aspect of the sacrificial arrangements under the Mosaic administration of the covenant of grace. Consider for that purpose the tabernacle of worship and the sacrificial system that in itself anticipated the definitive sacrifice for sin that Christ would make. The details of what were to be followed in the offering of sacrifices of the various kinds that God had specified are spelled out minutely in the book of Leviticus. In the sixteenth chapter of that book detailed instructions are given regarding the

---

43. Murray, *Redemption*, 154.
44. Turretin, *Institutes*, 647, 651, 653.

annual Day of Atonement on which, on that day alone once a year, the high priest was to enter the most holy place where the ark of the covenant stood and where the unique glory of God shone, and on behalf of the people the priest was to sprinkle the blood of the offering on the mercy seat. On the southern wall of the tabernacle stood the lampstand with its seven lamps. That light was necessary because the interior of the tabernacle would generally be darkened by reason of the curtain hangings that were part of its construction. But another aspect of the function of the lampstand is of particular significance.

The lampstand, standing where it was adjacent to the entrance to the most holy place, provided light for the high priest as on that solemn occasion once a year he entered the most holy place. The immediate relevance of that is that we can see in it a very significant anticipation of the office and function of Christ. Christ came to be the light. He came into the world as "the true Light which lighteth every man" (John 1:9). In that respect it is true that in one way or another, by the administration of his common grace to all men in general, and more significantly by his endowment of saving grace to his people, he is the true light. Profoundly, "God, who commanded the light to shine out of darkness [at the first creation], hath shined in our hearts, to give the light of the knowledge of the glory of God in the face of Jesus Christ" (2 Cor 4:6).

But as the lampstand of old lighted the way into the most holy presence of God, so now Christ, in the fact that he is the light, lights the way into the most holy place that is for us the very presence of God where his glory shines. For he himself is the High Priest who has entered the heavens before us and who now brings us to the Father on whose right hand he sits as our mediator and intercessor. "Seeing then that we have a great high priest, that is passed into the heavens, Jesus the Son of God . . . let us therefore come boldly unto the throne of grace, that we may obtain mercy, and find grace to help in time of need" (Heb 4:14–16).

The way opens, then, for a consideration of how, in fact, in all of what was involved in making such glorious provisions for his people, Christ fulfilled its requirements and necessities. We confront again the questions of "Why did Jesus Christ come into the world?" and what is it in which the highest privileges and benefits that become the property of his redeemed people consist? We meditate on the glory of Christ and what he has done for the rescue of sinners and their reconciliation with God, and the lines of John Henry Newman's hymn ring clear to us: "O loving wisdom of our

God! / When all was sin and shame, / A second Adam to the fight / And to the rescue came."[45]

We begin in the following chapter to confront the actions of Christ that are involved and the high themes related to the Christian believer's status and prospects.

---

45. Newman, "Praise to the Holiest in the height." In *Congregational Praise*, 71.

three

The Coming of Christ

Various answers, each in its context communicating a necessary aspect of Christian doctrine, have been given to the question: "Why did Jesus Christ come into the world?" We have already taken note of some of those answers, and when we considered the priestly office of Christ in the preceding chapter we saw some aspects of the meaning of the great exchange that his coming involved; the imputation of the guilt of the sinner's sin to Christ and the imputation of the forensic righteousness of Christ to the sinner. We shall address in this chapter two further aspects of the significance of what the redemption that Christ accomplished involved.

We have seen that in their ignorant and careless rejection of their Savior, the Jews of his day "by wicked hands" (Acts 2:23), by the cooperation of the Romans, crucified and put to death "the Lord of glory" (1 Cor 2:8). The two aspects of his redemptive accomplishment that we now address we may refer to as negative on the one hand and positive on the other. On the negative level we shall be occupied with what the Scriptures declare as the defeat and destruction of the devil and his works. We have it at 1 John 3:8 that "For this purpose the Son of God was manifested, that he might destroy the works of the devil." And the letter to the Hebrews states that the Son of God came into the world "that through death he might destroy him that had the power of death, that is, the devil" (Heb 2:14). On the positive level we shall endeavor to throw some light on the capstone of our Lord's redemptive objective in his statement that "I am come that they [the sheep of whom I am the good shepherd] might have life and might have it more

The Christian's Highest Good

abundantly" (John 10:10). The destruction of the devil and his domain and works on the one hand, and the elevation to the highest status of eternal life of the people whom God the Father gave to his Son to redeem on the other, hold within them the meaning of what the Son of God came into the world to do. Together, they span the scope of divine intent in the provision of redemption. We address the first of those levels first.

In relation to our Lord's redemptive objectives it is to be noted at the outset that in the discharge of his messianic-redemptive assignment Jesus Christ suffered and died for his people *in his human nature*. Of course his divine nature was engaged in many of his actions. It is to be said that those actions that were directly attributable to his divine nature were, ipso facto, attributable to his Person. For example, "If I with the finger of God cast out devils, no doubt the kingdom of God is come upon you" (Luke 11:20). And similarly, those actions that were directly attributable to his human nature were attributable to his Person. For example, "Jesus wept" (John 11:35). And given that our Lord was from the beginning of his ministry endowed with the Spirit "without measure" (John 3:34), it is properly said that all that he did while he was in this world was done in and with the strength of the Holy Spirit. We shall see that it was the presence of the Holy Spirit that supported and sustained his human nature as he bore the agonies of human soul in his death on the cross. "Through the eternal Spirit [he] offered himself without spot to God" (Heb 9:14). There was a communication between the divine and the human minds in his Person.

The humanity of Christ and the fact that it was in his human nature that he suffered and died is underlined by the reality of his temptations. He came, as is again clearly observable in the Scriptures, as the Second Adam, our first parent Adam being, as is said, "the figure [or the type] of him that was to come" (Rom 5:14; see also 1 Cor 15:45, 47). Sin had entered the world in human nature (Rom 5:12), and the guilt of Adam's first sin was imputed immediately (not mediately) to all his posterity who would descend from him by ordinary generation.[1] Adam had failed to honor the terms of his probation, and the covenant of works whose obligations he repudiated thenceforth remained obligatory on all who would come after him. It is to be grasped, therefore, that the reason for Christ's coming into the world was that he should do for his people what they were obligated to do under the covenant of works but what, by reason of their bondage to Satan and sin, they were unable to do for themselves. We may see in that

---

1. Westminster Shorter Catechism, Question 16.

The Coming of Christ

way the heavy responsibilities that rested on Christ, as in his human nature and in his probation that corresponded to the initial probationary status of the first Adam he confronted the devil. Our first parent failed in that probationary confrontation, but it is the glory of the gospel that the Second Adam did not fail. We have noted that John Henry Newman captured the reality in his verse: "O loving wisdom of our God! / When all was sin and shame, / A second Adam to the fight / And to the rescue came."[2]

But in that deeply significant situation, the reality of our Lord's temptations (both in the wilderness following his baptism and throughout his earthly life) speaks clearly to his humanity. For consider Satan's attack on our Lord's integrity. Satan could not tempt Christ as God. He once tempted God, and the result was that he was cast out of heaven and would finally be cast into eternal hell. No further attack on Jesus Christ as God could have any different effect or outcome. But Satan could and did tempt and attack the Savior of sinners in his human nature.

Our Lord's constitution in divine and human nature requires us to project our minds forward to look at the transactions between the Father and the Son when, on the cross, the penalty of sin was paid for the people whom Christ redeemed (John 17:6, 9). Again we hold foremost in mind that it was in his human nature that Christ died. He could not die in his divine nature. But now two issues come to bear on our understanding of what was necessary to the accomplishment of our redemption. First, we need to consider in what respect our Lord defeated Satan on the cross; and second, we should contemplate the respects in which Satan at that time did, in fact, know that he had been defeated.

What, then, was involved in the substitutionary death of Christ? The answer calls for the realization that on the cross our Lord suffered, *in human soul and in human body*. Prominently, it has to be said, he suffered in human soul in that he bore the agonies of eternal death, he passed through the pains of eternal death, and when he had triumphed over it and emerged victorious, and when the smile of the Father had returned to him, he voluntarily gave up his human soul to the Father and died his temporal death.[3] That temporal death was our Lord's final act of active obedience in keeping the law. For the law had said that the guilty one must die. And Christ on the cross was guilty, not of his own sin, for he had no sin, but of the sin of his people that he bore on their behalf. God the Father had *constituted* him

---

2. Newman, op. cit.
3. See the valuable discussion in Martin, *The Abiding Presence*, 132–40.

guilty by imputing our sin to him, and as we have seen, on the grounds of that constituting the Father could truthfully *declare* the Son guilty and lay upon him the penalty due to the sin he bore. The blood of Christ that atones for sin, our Lord's dying of natural human death, attains its efficacy by reason that it was the blood of One who, in passing triumphantly through the agonies of hell in human soul, had defeated the devil at that very point. We continue to hold to the truth that it was in his human nature that our Lord suffered and died. At that point we recognize the profound import of the statement that it was "through the [Holy] Spirit that he offered himself without spot to God" (Heb 9:14).

We ask, then, how did the devil know that he had been finally defeated? We might conjure a twofold answer. First, the devil, though as a created being his knowledge is not infinite, could observe God's election to eternal redemption of the host that he had given to his Son. The devil could not cause any alteration to the foreordained number or identity of that elect. But he could throughout their lives tempt and torture them (to the limit of God the Father's permission) and do all that was possible with his minions and confederate fallen angels to rob them of the joys of their salvation, if not pull them down to hell with him. But the time came, when Christ had accomplished his final act of redemption, when Satan saw and knew that he had lost all possibility of control over them. Christ, by his death, had definitively taken them out of the Satanic kingdom of darkness and had definitively saved them. They now belonged to Christ. They were now eternally his. They had been "bought with a price" (1 Cor 6:20). As the apostle Peter put it, they had been redeemed "not with corruptible things such as silver and gold . . . but with the precious blood of Christ" (1 Pet 1:18–19). Satan saw that he had lost them. By Christ's definitive redemption they now belonged eternally to him.

But secondly, Satan knew his final defeat when he observed that Christ, as has been said, passed triumphantly through the pains of hell when he bore the agonies of death in human soul on behalf of his people. He descended into hell on the cross. In his death, Christ actually saved his people. He did not die simply to make salvation possible. We do not hold a possibility theory of salvation, where salvation is understood to turn on a person's sovereign choice-decision to accept or reject the salvation that Christ made possible. We do not hold to any theory of a universal or indiscriminate atonement. We hold, to the contrary, to a biblical doctrine of particular atonement and to the fact that in that atonement Christ definitively saved his people. At the same time we do hold to an indiscriminate offer of the gospel, on the grounds of the invitation of our Lord himself that whosoever will may come to him and partake of the waters of life freely (Rev 22:17). All who hear the gospel *may* come to Christ. But, it might be responded, *who will?* And the eternally ordained answer follows that only those *will* who have been made the beneficiaries of God's sovereignly distributed grace of regeneration. "All that the Father giveth me shall come to me" (John 6:37), our Lord said, and he added that "No man can come to me except the Father which hath sent me draw him" (John 6:44). The sovereignty and the mercy of God are in full display at every stage of the definitive redemption of sinners.

The defeat of Satan by our Lord's redemptive work is thus final, definitive, and sure. True it is, as we have seen, that at God's permission the devil can still torture the saints and interrupt and tarnish their relations with God the Father, but as Martin Luther's famous hymn has it, "his doom is sure."[4] The reality of the Christian's status is that he has been "delivered from the power of darkness [from the satanic regime of condemnation and death] into the kingdom of [God's] dear Son" (Col 1:13).

The Works of the Devil

The aged apostle John, looking back over a long life of pastoral ministry, was able to speak knowingly of the fact that Jesus Christ came into the world "that he might destroy the works of the devil" (1 John 3:8). He had seen that happen in the lives of the "children" to whom he wrote. We have observed that not only the works of the devil, but the devil himself, have been destroyed, as the writer to the Hebrews explained (Heb 2:14). What, then, is to be said of the "works of the devil?" The answer resides on two distinct, but related levels.

First, it was the work of the devil that trapped our first parents into their sinful repudiation of their covenantal obligations to God. Satan, whose original perfidy had cast him out of heaven, set out to mar, to disfigure, and to corrupt, if not to destroy, the handiwork of God in the universe of reality that he had spoken into existence. The record of the human fall into sin is well known. But what it involved was the loss of our first parents' original holiness and knowledge of God and, as the Catechism puts it, "the corruption of their whole nature, which is commonly called original

---

4. Luther, "A Mighty Fortress Is Our God," in *Trinity Hymnal*, 92.

sin."⁵ Two results followed. First, as is observable more expansively in the scriptural data, the guilt of Adam's first sin (not his subsequent sins) was imputed immediately (not mediately) to all those who would descend from him by ordinary generation. And second, it followed that there occurred a transmission of fallen nature to all that natural posterity. There occurred, in our first parents' fall, both a *deprivation*, in the loss of original holy standing before God, and a *depravation*, in that the faculties of human soul were now depraved and disabled as to the possibility of knowing God, or of regaining eternal life and felicity by obeying God. We speak properly of the natural man's total depravity, meaning by that not that he is now as evil as he could possibly be. That will have become true following the crack of doom, when, at the day of judgment, the common grace of God has come to an end. But now the faculties of soul, though they have not in themselves been destroyed (fallen man can still think and love and act with the volition of free agency)—the faculties of soul have been disabled from their pristine efficiency in knowing, enjoying communion with, and honoring God their maker. All men are now "born in sin and shapen in iniquity" (Ps 51:5). As to the intellectual faculty, "the god of this world has blinded the mind" (2 Cor 4:4). As to the faculty of affection, "the heart is deceitful above all things and desperately wicked" (Jer 17:9). "God saw that the wickedness of man was great in the earth, and that every imagination of the thoughts of his heart was only evil continually" (Gen 6:5). So it has continued in the natural progeny of Adam, except the renewing grace of God intervenes. And as to the faculty of will, man has become the slave and dupe of the devil (John 8:44; Luke 11:21–22). "He that committeth sin is of the devil" (1 John 3:8). Such is the sorry state to which the fall reduced mankind.

But secondly, of immediate and pressing importance is the impact of the "works of the devil" in and on the lives, not only of mankind in general, but also of the people of God, those who have been renewed in being and character by the regenerating grace of God's Holy Spirit. It is the more necessary to take cognizance of that dimension because of what is to be said in a moment regarding the reason for Christ's coming into the world; namely to give life, and life "more abundantly," to the people whom, by his saving work, he redeemed.

This world, Martyn Lloyd-Jones observed, "has become the kingdom of Satan."⁶ Satan is "the god of this world" (2 Cor 4:4). And men need to

---

5. Westminster Shorter Catechism, Question 18.
6. See the valuable discussion in Lloyd-Jones, *Children of God*, 59–70.

The Coming of Christ

be delivered from that Satanic kingdom. They need, by the grace of God to be "delivered from the power of darkness and translated into the kingdom of God's dear Son" (Col 1:13). It was precisely that that Jesus Christ came into the world to do. How, then, does that come to effect? Our Lord himself explained the outcome when he said that "When a strong man armed [the devil] keepeth his palace, his goods [the souls of men whom he keeps in the slumber of sin and unrighteousness] are in peace; But when a stronger than he [the Lord Jesus Christ] shall come upon him, and overcome him, he taketh from him all his armour wherein he trusted, and divideth his spoils" (Luke 11:21–22).

But what of the lives and experience of those among men who, by God's redemptive grace, belong to him? What, if any, are the "works of the devil" that are relevant to them? At this crucial point the entire questions of the means and the progress of God's people in sanctification are at issue. In our present space a brief number of headings can be noted.

First, the attacks of Satan on the grounds of the believer's assurance of his adoption into the family of God are all too clearly rampant. While Satan, as he knows, cannot dislodge the Christian from the status of definitive redemption by God's grace, he can, as he sets out to do, disturb the peace and confidence of the child of God. He can for the moment entice and trap the true child of God into occasions of sin, though he knows that he no longer has his erstwhile dominion over him. Satan's task, as he himself sees it, is to make the Christian believer miserable, to rob him, not of his salvation, but of the joy of his salvation. Why does the Christian sin? we ask. Whence his thoughts of evil, rather than good? The source is satanic impulse. The enemy of our souls plants the imaginations of evil even in sanctified hearts, and for a time draws the soul away from the path of righteousness. What, then, is the Christian's remedy? The apostle John again understood the complex of human life and possibilities on those levels. The highest privilege of the Christian, he explained, is "fellowship with the Father" (1 John 1:3–7), and when Satan has attacked, when the integrity of one's walk with God has faltered, the way of recovery is clear: "If we confess our sins, he is faithful and just to forgive us our sins, and to cleanse us from all unrighteousness" (1 John 1:9). For "if we walk in the light, as he is in the light, we have fellowship one with another [that is, fellowship between the Christian believer and his God]" (1 John 1:7). And the ground on which that is possible is that "the blood of Jesus Christ his Son cleanseth us from all sin" (1 John 1:7).

Second, it is the work of the devil to discourage the Christian in his attention to the means of grace and, as a result, from his diligence in the pursuit of sanctification. Are we at any time and in any respect less than diligent in prayer? Do we become delinquent in attention to the word of God? Is his word to us the very word of life and food to the soul? Do we allow his word to direct our steps? What of our cultivation of the benefits of attendance at the house of God and the communion of the saints? Do we recall that the troubled believer in Psalm 73 understood his situation and the condition of the world that had perplexed him when he "went into the sanctuary of God" (Ps 73:17)? The questions that impinge on the possible states of the Christian soul, and the devil's success in derailing the Christian life for a time, could be multiplied. The answers that must be given to such questions are clear to the practiced Christian.

Third, Satan too easily diverts our gaze from the things of God, from the beauty of the culture of the kingdom of God, to the things, the mores, the habits and the life-patterns of the culture of the world. We are members, of necessity, of the "common kingdom" of humanity in which God has left us to live until the great day of his appearing, but we are citizens also of the redemptive kingdom of God. The devil would blur or break down in our consciousness the boundaries between the world and the church into which we have been called by the grace of God. It is our task to be diligent in understanding the distinctions that God has established, and which we are to preserve, between the culture of the world and the culture of the church. The ways in which the "works of the devil" interfere with our perceptions on those important levels will again be clear to the attentive and reflective Christian believer.

Life More Abundantly

We observed that the reason for Jesus Christ's coming into the world was to be addressed in our present brief terms under two heads. First he came, as we have seen, to destroy "the works of the devil." And second, he came in order that the people whom he redeemed "might have life and have it more abundantly." The first of those reasons we suggested was to be understood as negative. We turn now to the positive reason, which takes up the life-giving power of the work and redemptive accomplishment of Christ. We shall address that more extensively in the following chapters.

The conception of "life more abundantly" takes up all that is involved in the believer's knowledge and assurance of salvation, as that turns on the redemptive accomplishment of Christ on his behalf. It involves forgiveness of sin and reconciliation with God. "Being justified by faith we have peace with God" (Rom 5:1). Now, that is to say, God is at peace with his people. The existential implications are extensive, and the meaning and implications for life of what is at issue can be addressed only briefly at this introductory stage.

When we referred to the distribution of redemptive offices among the Persons of the Godhead before the foundation of the world, we observed that the redemptive office of the Holy Spirit is to convey to those for whom Christ died the gifts and benefits that he purchased for them. Among those benefits particularly are the gifts of saving faith and repentance. That deposit of gifts occurs at the point of the conveyance to the soul by the Holy Spirit of the grace of regeneration. It is all too true that the Spirit of God may, and does, depending on his sovereign purpose, work his influence within the soul of an individual, in conviction of sin and of one's obligation to God, without necessarily conveying to that person the grace of regeneration. Great, indeed, is the mystery of godliness (1 Tim 3:16) and the mystery of the sovereign activity of God by his Spirit in the souls of men. The opening paragraph of the sixth chapter of the letter to the Hebrews provides an illuminating instance. Those referred to there, notwithstanding the extensive work and influence of the Holy Spirit of which they were the beneficiaries, remained in an unregenerate state.[7]

God's grace of regeneration is conceived of in scriptural terms in several ways. For example: "God who commanded the light to shine out of darkness [at the first creation]," it is said, "hath shined in our hearts to give the light of the knowledge of the glory of God in the face of Jesus Christ" (2 Cor 4:6). "You hath he quickened, who were dead in trespasses and sins" (Eph 2:1), invoking the fifth verse of the same chapter – "When we were dead in our sins [he] hath quickened us together with Christ." And "if any

---

7. It is of interest that the well-known and prolific author R. C. Sproul rejects that conclusion regarding the sixth chapter of the letter to the Hebrews. Sproul observes: "If repentance is, as Reformed theology believes, a fruit of regeneration, then the author of Hebrews is describing people who have been regenerated. . . . This reference to repentance convinces me that the author is describing regenerate Christians," *Grace Unknown*, 214. Sproul has failed to see that the text in view is speaking of the impossibility of renewing the people the author has in view to the false repentance they had previously made. The author of Hebrews therefore sets them aside and proceeds to speak of, and to, God's people.

man be in Christ, he is a new creature; old things are passed away, all things are become new" (2 Cor 5:17).

At the point of regeneration, and proceeding in God's ordination from the grace of regeneration, is a profoundly meaningful threefold blessing. First, by that work of the Spirit of God an individual is the recipient of what is referred to in biblical-doctrinal terms as the baptism of [or with or by] the Holy Spirit. "For by one Spirit are we all baptized into one body" (1 Cor 12:13). It is not necessary to digress at this point to reflect on the gross misunderstandings regarding the baptism of the Spirit that abound in the confessing church. Suffice it to say that in this we have the first of the three important benefits that accrue in the act of regeneration.

Second, in his regeneration an individual is the beneficiary of the sealing of [or by] the Spirit. That is to be understood as the meaning of the statement in a somewhat disputed text in Paul's letter to the Ephesians, "In whom [Christ] also after that ye believed ye were sealed with that holy Spirit of promise" (Eph 1:13). Again the doctrine of the sealing of the Spirit has been variously understood, and again the true benefit of it is evacuated if it is not understood to be the gracious act of God when, in regenerating the sinner, he places upon him his seal of ownership and property. That divine seal of ownership is referred to again in the same letter to the Ephesians when Paul cautions his readers: "Grieve not the holy Spirit of God, whereby ye are sealed unto the day of redemption" (Eph 4:30). Again it is not necessary to digress at this time to address the confusions of doctrine that have arisen at this singularly important point.

Third, and in this we come to a highly important implication of the Holy Spirit's work of regeneration, by that act of grace the individual is joined in union to Christ. The profound doctrine of the believer's union with Christ beckons our careful understanding, and what is involved can be put by saying that the believer is joined to Christ in an organic, vital, spiritual, and indissoluble union. Christ himself prayed to the Father in his high priestly prayer, "that they all may be one; as thou, Father, art in me, and I in thee, that they also may be one in us" (John 17:19–21). Further, Jesus said to one of his disciples during his Supper Discourses on the night of his betrayal, "If a man love me, he will keep my words; and my Father will love him, and *we* will come unto him, and make our abode with him" (John 14:23). The union with Christ implies and carries along with it union with the three Persons of the Godhead.[8] The individual does not become aware

---

8. See the valuable discussion in Murray, *Redemption*, 201–13.

of his union with Christ and begin to cultivate its significance until, with conscious awareness, he moves in faith toward conversion. One Reformed writer has observed that "The initial act is that of Christ, who unites believers to himself by regenerating them and thus producing faith in them. On the other hand, the believer also unites himself to Christ by a conscious act of faith, and continues the union, under the influence of the Holy Spirit, by the constant exercise of faith."[9]

The doctrine of the Christian believer's union with Christ casts back to the deliberations of the Godhead before the foundation of the world, to the election of the subjects of the covenant of redemption. For at that point "The God and Father of our Lord Jesus Christ . . . hath chosen us in him . . . having predestinated us unto the adoption of children by Jesus Christ to himself" (Eph 1:3–5). The reality of our union with Christ, therefore, embraces the full range of benefits that accrue to the Christian believer. In the light of the believer's union with Christ, it is to be said not only that he now lives his new life in Christ and that Christ lives in him by his Holy Spirit, but that all that happened to Christ in the processes of redemption happened to him. When Christ died, he died. When Christ rose again, he rose with him. And further, God has "raised us up together, and made us to sit together in heavenly places in Christ Jesus" (Eph 2:6). The astounding thought speaks to the highest of the privileges that have accrued to the Christian believer. And as to life in this world, "I am crucified with Christ," the apostle said, "nevertheless I live; yet not I, but Christ liveth in me; and the life which I now live in the flesh I live by the faith of [in] the Son of God, who loved me, and gave himself for me" (Gal 2:20).

The union with Christ is an organic union because it absorbs the Christian into an organic entity, the organism of the church of which Christ is the Head. That reality lies behind the statement that the union with Christ is a vital union. It is vital in that it is the source and origin of the vitality of life that characterizes the individual Christian. In the same sense it has been defined as a spiritual union. That is so because it is the Holy Spirit himself who activates and sustains the union. From the grounding of the union, from its preservation by the Spirit, and from the guarantee that our Lord himself has given on the basis of it, the union is indissoluble.

Our Lord said in his discourse on his identity as the good shepherd that he knows "his own sheep by name," that "I am the good shepherd and know my sheep," that "I lay down my life for the sheep," and that, therefore,

---

9. Berkhof, op. cit., 450.

The Christian's Highest Good

"I give unto them eternal life; and they shall never perish, neither shall any man pluck them out of my hand" (John 10:3, 14, 15, 28). Union with Christ, in its manifold implications for the being and the life-journey of the Christian, is of the highest of blessings that are bestowed with Christian identity. We reflect on the sorry lapse of Adam's fall and its bequest to all mankind that followed from him. Now by the grace of regeneration, not only does the individual who is the beneficiary of it live in newness of life and enjoy the considerable benefits we have observed, but beyond that, he is joined to Christ. Regeneration does not simply raise the Christian again to the place and status that Adam enjoyed before he fell. We have it from the apostle at Romans 5:20 that "where sin abounded, grace did much more abound." Sin abounded when Adam fell. And grace abounded to overcome the effects of the fall. But the statement before us is that grace *more abounded*. The *more abounded* is declared in the fact that now the Christian is raised to a much higher state than that from which Adam fell. He is raised to a state of indissoluble union with Christ himself. Adam was not joined to Christ in that respect. He was in his created state holy; it was possible for him not to sin, but he was mutable, defectible, and capable of falling. Now that the believer is joined in indissoluble union to Christ it is not possible for him to fall. That is the higher estate to which he has been raised.

But beyond all that has been said, the final and highest meaning of our Lord's statement that he came to give his people "life more abundantly" rests in the fact, as the apostle John again stated it, that the Christian believer now has "fellowship with God" (1 John 1:3, 7). That is the Christian's highest privilege. Not only is he or she a child of God (John 1:12; Rom 8:16–17), adopted into the family of God (Gal 4:5; Rom 8:15), but the Christian has immediate access to God the Father and communion with him. Now the Christian comes freely into the very throne room of heaven. Through Christ, Paul concluded, "we have access by one Spirit unto the Father" (Eph 2:18). It is our high privilege now to "come boldly unto the throne of grace, that we may obtain mercy, and find grace to help in time of need" (Heb 5:16).

When we speak of the believer's adoption into the family of God, a benefit, we have said, that is integral with, or consequent upon, the Holy Spirit's conveyance to an individual of the grace of regeneration, it is necessary to maintain in that respect an important point of biblical doctrine. We observe, though we leave the issue less than fully developed for our present purpose, that the justification of the believer on the exercise of the gifts of repentance and faith that have been conveyed to him in his regeneration involves a forensic, declarative statement by God. It is forensic in that it effects a definitive change in the believer's status in relation to the law of God. Justification does not, in itself, cause or imply any change in the individual's state of holiness. It is purely a statement by God that whereas previously the individual was *ungodly*, in that he had not kept the law, he is now deemed in the accounting of God to be *godly*, because the fact that Christ kept the law on his behalf has been imputed to him, or placed to his account. The change in state that renders the person holy is referable not to his justification but to his regeneration. Justification is simply and purely forensic.

That having been said, what, then, is to be said of the believer's adoption, his adoption into the family of God? Are we to understand that God's act of adoption is also essentially forensic, that its explanation is to be found primarily in its implied change in legal status? John Murray has observed that "Adoption is, like justification, a judicial act. . . . it is the bestowal of a status, or standing, not the generating within us of a new nature or character."[10] Such a statement might be thought to imply that emphasis should fall on the forensic significance of the act of adoption. But Murray, though he insists that adoption is to be distinguished from both justification and regeneration and "is much more than either or both of these acts of grace,"[11] goes on to observe that "There is a close relation between adoption and regeneration."[12] Careful thought should be given, therefore, to working out the relations that are in view at those points. It is true that regeneration involves a change in moral nature, while adoption involves the establishment of a new and living relation between God and the regenerate believer. But in view of the distinctions that Murray has raised, and in view of the relations involved in the total application of redemption, it is necessary to avoid the conclusion that adoption is, like justification, a purely forensic act.

We have it in Galatians 4:5 that Christ redeemed us in order that "we might receive the adoption of sons [or as sons]," or, in the instance we are now considering, the adoption that properly belongs to sons. It is as sons that we are adopted, with full rights to all the privileges and benefits of sonship. And at the same time we have received also "the Spirit of adoption" (Rom 8:15), who applies to us the realization of the benefits and privileges

10. Murray, *Redemption*, 166.
11. Ibid., 165.
12. Ibid., 166.

that adoption implies. God gives the believer, that is, both the new status of adoption into sonship and the "Spirit of adoption" who makes that status meaningful and operative in the life of the believer.

But we avoid the conclusion that the high status of adoption proceeds from a purely forensic statement by God. It is to be seen as associated with the believer's regeneration, and integral to the complex of God's actions in relation to the complete application of redemption. Adoption is an act of God's grace that is an integral aspect of, and by inevitable implication follows from, regeneration. God the Father does not adopt us to make us sons. Because, according to his eternal ordination, he "gave us power to become the sons of God" (John 1:12), he has adopted us as sons. We are not sons because we have adopted. We have been adopted because God has made us sons.

That important point of doctrine should be carefully understood. The distinction is frequently drawn between one who is a son in a certain family by natural birth, on the one hand, and one who has been transferred to become a son of a different family by adoption. In the eyes of the law, then, the one who has been adopted has a right to all the benefits and privileges of membership of the family into which he has been adopted. In that way, the law is casting its judgment on the case, and that means that the forensic aspect of the adoption is predominant. But in the case we have under examination, namely adoption into the family of God, that legal principle and relationship should not be allowed to assume initial prominence. For it must be understood that as to the matter of sonship of God, the Christian believer, who has a right to all the benefits and privileges of membership of the family of God, *is a son by birth*. That is the critical factor in the case. The Christian believer is *a son of God by birth* because he has been *born again* by the Spirit of God. And because his status as a son turns in that manner on the new identity that the Holy Spirit of God produces within him, the individual now partakes of the nature of his heavenly Father. It is precisely that emergence, by the grace and by the fact of regeneration, of the very nature of God that is thereby conveyed to the sinner that raises the identity of sonship far above that of a mere forensic relationship. Nothing less than what has now been stated is involved in the Holy Spirit's conveyance to God's chosen people of the grace of regeneration. That is why John can say that "we are the sons of God" (1 John 3:2). The necessary linkage of the doctrine and fact of our adoption to the reality of regeneration has been well stated by Joel Beeke: "*When we are born again*, Christ delivers us from Satan's slavery, and ... transfers us to the Father's sonship.... The Holy Spirit changes us from children of wrath, which we are by nature, into children of God by means of regeneration, or the new birth, sealing our adoption with His own witness."[13] Candlish observes: "Literally and truly he [God] begets us as children to himself."[14] And then, because we are the sons of God, we are joint-heirs with Christ (Rom 8:16–17).

A final comment is necessary at this preliminary stage by way of addressing the fact that Christ came into the world in order that his people might have life more abundantly. The apex of the benefits involved rests in the fact that the believer now has "fellowship with the Father, and with his Son, Jesus Christ" (1 John 1:3). God is not distant from those he has assumed into sonship. They are "the apple of his eye" (Zech 2:8). He calls them to intimate communion with himself, for he says to them that "I have loved thee with an everlasting love; therefore with lovingkindness have I drawn thee" (Jer 31:3). That high privilege of fellowship with the Father depends upon, and it follows from, the fact that the Christian believer knows God as his Father for who he is. The apostle John, who had quoted in his gospel our Lord's intention that his people should have life more abundantly, has summed up the meaning and the reality of it as follows: "We know that the Son of God is come, and hath given us an understanding, that we may know him that is true, even in his Son Jesus Christ" (1 John 5:20). Christ came, that is, to give us an understanding. The believer knows and understands things that were previously completely alien to him. Fellowship with God involves an intellectual awareness. In terms that apply to all of the believer's relations with God, on all of the levels on which those relations exist and are operative, the whole person, with all the faculties of soul that define him, is engaged.

But life more abundantly carries with it also the profound eschatological prospect that has been accorded the sons of God. It is not necessary to expand at this point all that involves. We have explored all too briefly something of the benefits that have even now accrued to the Christian believer. He now rejoices in Christ "with joy unspeakable and full of glory" (1 Pet 1:8); he rests in the knowledge and assurance that "now are we the sons of God, and it doth not yet appear what we shall be; but we know that when he shall appear we shall be like him; for we shall see him as he is" (1 John 3:2).

---

13. Beeke, "The Apostle John and the Puritans on the Father's Adopting, Transforming Love" in Beeke, *The Beauty and Glory of the Father*, 86, 89, italics added.

14. Candlish, *Commentary*, 193.

And the Christian knows that he will live and reign with his Lord when he enters into his eschatological kingdom, when "in the dispensation of the fullness of times [God will] gather together in one all things in Christ" (Eph 1:10). All that is part of the "life more abundantly" that the Savior of men came to give to his people.

We shall expand further in the following chapter on the Christian's privilege of fellowship with the Father that is, as we shall explore the blessings it conveys, the Christian's highest good.

Conclusion

What, in summary, are we to understand as the reason "Why Jesus Christ came into the world?" We have crystallized the answer and explanation by observing that the purpose in Christ's coming was twofold: first, to destroy the works of the devil and to destroy the devil himself; and second, to establish the grounds and considerations on which the people that God the Father gave to him to redeem "might have life and have it more abundantly."

That twofold reality encapsulates for the Christian the meaning and privileges of the new life in Christ to which, by the sovereign and electing grace of God he has been introduced and in which he has been incorporated. The Christian's *summum bonum* is to see God. We do not now see him with the eyes of flesh. But we shall see him in the last great day in seeing our Lord in glorified state, when we shall see him as he is and shall be like him (1 John 3:1–2). In this life, with eyes of flesh we cannot *see* God, but we can *know* God (John 17:3), and now, while we walk by his grace through this short, uncertain life and earthly pilgrimage, existentially conscious of our mystical, spiritual, but absolute union with him, we have fellowship with him, with God his Son, Jesus Christ, and with God the Holy Spirit.

The devoted Christian exclaims with the apostle: "Thanks be unto God for his unspeakable gift" (2 Cor 9:15). That gift, none other than God's own dear Son, transports the Christian believer, not only to a state of comfort in the knowledge, and even the assurance, of sins forgiven, but through Christ our mediator to the very throne room of heaven. May we by his grace yet learn to live to his glory in the shortening days he has reserved for us.

four

The Christian's Highest Good

Our objective in this and the following chapters is to expand what has already been said regarding the reason for Christ's coming into the world and to reflect further on the implications that his coming has for the Christian life. Two principal questions will occupy our discussion. First, as a result of the redemption that Christ accomplished, what is to be understood as the Christian's highest good; and second, how is that reflected in the identity of the confessing Christian and, as a result, in his or her actual life and behavior?

What has just been said implies that when we refer to the Christian's highest good we do not have in view what we have referred to previously as the ultimate *summum bonum*, or the highest good as that will be realized when, in the day of our Lord's appearing, the Christian sees God as he is in his glorified Son. We shall see him in his glorified human nature, as he had prayed to the Father on the night on which he was betrayed: "And now, O Father, glorify thou me with thine own self, with the glory which I had with thee before the world was" (John 17:5). But we are concerned now with the Christian's highest good as that is realizable in this present life. In one respect, that highest good, as it is presently the Christian's possession, is to *know God*. "This is life eternal," John had said in his gospel, "that they might *know thee*, the only true God" (John 17:3). Highly significant though the Christian's knowledge of God is, and while it is the distinguishing reality that separates the Christian from all other people, much more is involved. And it was to address that "much more" in a consistent and extended manner that the apostle John wrote his First Epistle. That highest good was identified in the preceding chapter in the words of John as "fellowship with the Father." "Truly our fellowship is with the Father, and with his Son Jesus Christ" (1 John 1:3). But, we now ask, what does that fellowship mean and imply and confer on the Christian as he works his way through the uncertain days of his pilgrimage in this world? It will provide perspective for what follows to observe the way in which the apostle John unfolds the argument of his epistle, as he maintains his initial proposition and examines its implications.

What lies before us in more detail can be summarized in three questions: First, who is it with whom the fellowship of which we are speaking is possible? Second, what are the grounds on which that fellowship has become possible? And third, what is to be said of the character of those who are the beneficiaries of that high privilege of fellowship?

The Holiness of God

At the end of a long life of pastoral ministry John sets out for his readers what he wishes them to understand as the essence of the gospel as he had received that from the Lord himself, and what, in the light of that, they should embrace and cultivate as the highest blessings and privileges accorded them as Christian people. The syntactical structure of the first verse of John's letter is expressive. He begins with the words: "That which was from the beginning, which we have heard . . ." It appears that John is about to set out what it was that he had heard. But he digresses in order to speak of "the Word of life," the Lord Jesus Christ, the Second Person of the Godhead who had come in the flesh, and with whom he and the other disciples had traveled and from whom they had learned. In that important and necessary digression John placed before his readers the Person of Christ in both his *essential* or eternal identity and his *incarnate* or *official* or *redemptive identity* to which we shall return in a moment.

But after his digression John returns to his "That which we have heard" in the third verse of his first chapter, and in the fifth verse he lays out his answer to our first question. "This then is the message which we have heard of him" (1 John 1:5). "God," he says, "is light." The basic datum, which provides the ground for all of the reasoning that will follow in his letter, is that God is a holy God. That is the issue in brief. God is light. God is holy, and in him is no darkness. But John's conception is at that point widened. He makes it clear that the "fellowship with the Father," that provides the frame

The Christian's Highest Good

within which all that he will go on to say is to be read and understood, carries with it "fellowship with his Son Jesus Christ" (1 John 1:3).

That latter statement is pregnant with meaning. It is not being said simply that there exists in some sense the possibility of fellowship with the Father and also with the Son on separate and differing levels. There are clearly respects in which that is true.[1] But at this initial stage of his letter John is saying something different. The fellowship of which he speaks, the significance and potential of which he will go on to elaborate, is with the Father and the Son together. That is clarified in the very last words of his letter, where he appeals to the Christian believer's union with the Father and the Son together as grounding all he has said to that point. He had spoken there of the fact that "We know that we are of God" (1 John 5:19), and from that, as John argued, the profound result has followed that "we are in him" (1 John 5:20). The profound statement is that the Christian believer is "in God," as John's context states. It is difficult to express that truth and its meaning in language that is at our command as finite persons; its truth lies on a level of fact and comprehension that only the Christian can begin to grasp. The hymn writer grasped something of its reality and significance when he said: "None but his loved ones know."[2]

But the reality is pressed on the Christian mind. The status to which the Christian believer has been raised by the regenerating grace of God implies nothing less than that. The Christian believer is now "in God." Then the explanation follows in the same verse: The Christian is "in his Son Jesus Christ" (1 John 5:20). The issue is that because of the Christian's union with Christ he has, at the same time and because of his union with the Son, union with the Father. Union with Christ, moreover, carries with it union with the three Persons of the Godhead. John's doctrine points clearly to the fact and the truth of the consubstantiality of the divine Persons, and it is therefore with them together that the fellowship of which John is speaking exists and transmits to the Christian the benefits that John goes on to display.

We have, as it were, "bookend" statements at the beginning and the end of John's letter. At the third verse of the first chapter he states his basic and orientating conception of fellowship with the Father and the Son. Then

---

1. Owen observes regarding the saints' "communion with God" that "in respect of the distinct persons of the Godhead with whom they have fellowship, it is either *distinct* and peculiar, or else obtained and exercised *jointly* and in common," in Owen, *Works*, 2:9.

2. The reference is to an eleventh-century Latin hymn translated by Edward Caswell in 1849. In *Trinity Hymnal*, 645.

The Christian's Highest Good

in the closing verses of the letter he returns for a final time to his principal theme. The fellowship is with the Father and the Son. The Christian is "in God," and he is "in the Son" (1 John 5:19–20). John will work out the details and the implications of that remarkable truth which, now in his closing days, has taken up the passion of his soul.

When John refers to "the Word of life" (1 John 1:1) we hear the echo of the prologue to his gospel. The Second Person of the Godhead is the "Word," as he was "the Word" at the very beginning of the creation when God spoke into existence all that exists external to the Godhead. "He ['the Word'] was God [and] was in the beginning with God. All things were made by him" (John 1:1–3). And "by him were all things created" (Col 1:16). The Second Person of the Godhead came into the world to "declare" God unto us. "No man hath seen God at any time; the only begotten Son, which is in the bosom of the Father, he hath declared him" (John 1:18). God has spoken by and through his Son. He has had no dealings with the human race except through his Son and the Holy Spirit whom his Son has sent to speak of him. Now in the opening statement of his letter John places before his readers that eternal or *essential* identity of the Son, and he immediately follows that by the statement that he was "manifested" to John and the disciples in ways that he indicates. We have referred at some length in chapter two to Christ's eternal or essential identity. At this point John emphasizes that the same Second Person of the Godhead actually came into the world, and in human nature walked and taught and revealed God and, in a manner that John will explain, provided redemption for his people through his substitutionary life and death. That, we shall see, takes up the reality of our Lord's incarnation, his presence in the world. We have referred at an earlier point to the miracles involved in our Lord's incarnation; the miracle of the breaking of the entailment of sin that was involved in the preparation of the virgin's womb, and that of the Holy Spirit's impregnation of the sanctified egg of the virgin.

The crux of John's epistle, and the coordinating motif of all of the argument and doctrinal analysis he sets forth in it, is found in his repeated claim that the Christian's highest good exists in the privilege of fellowship with the Father. Now in verse 5 of his first chapter he begins his fuller statement of the gospel in which that privilege and the benefits it conveys are stated. His statement is a remarkable portrayal of the essential terms of the gospel and the priorities implicit in it. The first statement of the gospel is, as John says, that "God is light." God is a holy God. But it is important to grasp the apostle's more complete claim at that point. The gospel is, of course, addressed to man in his miserable and lost state in sin. But we are told here that the first statement of the gospel, and what must therefore always be the first statement in the preaching of the gospel, is not a statement about man. The first statement is a statement about God, and a reminder that we and the whole world have to do with a holy God. We note here also that the first statement of the gospel is not about man's state in sin, or about Adam's fall that caused that estate. Nor is it a statement about the provision for redemption from sin that God has made. Those things are all, of course, critically important parts of the gospel, and they will follow later. But they must not be placed up front. They have no meaning and cannot be understood for what they are unless the first statement has been made perfectly clear. The first statement is that God is light and that he lives in light, and only then does John differentiate between the light in which God exists and the darkness that is man's natural state. And then only after that does he come in verse 7 to the fact that "the blood of Jesus Christ" has been set forth as a cleansing from sin. That order of statement is imperative.

But we must press the question, incomplete and insufficient though our answers will necessarily be. What is involved in the fellowship with the eternally holy God that is stated to us as the Christian's highest good? By virtue of the completed redemptive work of Christ we have access to the very presence of the Father. It was for precisely that reason and for that objective that the Father sent his Son into the world. We recall that before Adam fell into sin his fellowship with God was one of closest intimacy. God "walked with Adam in the garden in the cool of the day" (Gen 3:8). In that close communion God revealed to Adam the scope and purposes of the divine will in creation, he gave to Adam the laws and mandates by which he should live in order to please God, and he made clear to Adam the conditions on which, in his perseverance in obedience to God, he would inherit eternal life. By obedience, Adam would be confirmed in moral state and raised to eternal life and impeccability. Adam then, in the state of intrinsic holiness in which he had been created, knew and conversed with God in and with a naturalness that since his fall had been closed to all his posterity in their natural state. But now, we recall from previous exposition, the Christian believer has been raised, not simply to the state from which Adam fell, but to the much higher state of indissoluble union with the three Persons of the Godhead. It follows that there has again been opened to the Christian the privilege of close communion with the Father, even beyond the level of privilege that Adam enjoyed.

The Christian's Highest Good

The eternal Father is now father to the son, the Christian believer whom he has called and whom he has reconciled to himself. Now the son, the new-born child of God, can come to the throne of the Father and converse with him in closest intimacy. There is again a likeness of mind between the Father and the son, the child whom he has redeemed. The apostle Paul has summed up the state of relationship by saying that now "we have the mind of Christ" (1 Cor 2:16). The Christian has begun to see all things as God in Christ himself sees them, the being and glory of God, the meaning of sin, the Personhood of Christ who came to declare and represent the Father, and the meaning of redemption and reconciliation with God. We are careful to say that the Christian has *begun* to see all these things with, as it has been given to him, the mind of Christ. The process of the Christian's learning will continue to and beyond the end of his life-journey in this world. Eternity will not exhaust what is to be known of the glory to which the Christian has been introduced.

Fellowship with the Father means and implies that the Christian, who comes into the presence of the Father clothed with "the robe of righteousness" of Christ (Isa 61:10), can speak to the Father, and listen to the Father speaking to him, of the most intimate issues and cares of life. A perfect openness now exists between them. We are not speaking here of a mere non-rational mysticism. Admitted to the innermost holy place of the Father's presence, the Christian can come with all the faculties of human soul engaged. The Christian's communion with God is an intelligent communion. It is a communion grounded in a love for God that is breathed from the knowledge of reconciliation and sins forgiven. It is a communion that is free of inhibition because the volition that it exercises has itself been renewed and strengthened by the renewing, regenerating grace of God.

In fellowship with the Father, the Christian hears the Father speak again the words that he has already inscripturated in the Word that he has given. In hearing the Father speak those same words, and waiting as the Spirit of God by whom the Father speaks illumines the soul with recurring new levels of comprehension, the Christian relishes not only the comfort and safety of the Father's presence, but the calming peace of assurance of his heavenly Father's pleasure.

In the moments of communion with God that the Christian's status of fellowship with the Father permits, he knows something more of the meaning of "the love of God shed abroad in our hearts" (Rom 5:5). The Christian comes to the Father without cluttered inhibition, but with a reverence born of godly fear and worshipful praise and adoration. Admitted to the intimacies of fellowship, aspects of the mind and heart of God are disclosed to the Christian again, and the realization of the meaning of the Father's declaration is born afresh: "I have loved thee with an everlasting love; therefore with lovingkindness have I drawn thee" (Jer 31:3). But indeed, "great is the mystery of godliness" (1 Tim 3:16), and we pause to be reminded that it is by reason of our union with Christ, the eternal Son of God who came to reconcile us to the Father, that we have union with the three Persons of the Godhead. Our fellowship with the Father, grounded as it is in that realization, takes up the mediation and intercession for us of the eternal Son who is now discharging his heavenly high priestly office and function, and the impress on our souls of the Holy Spirit's mediation to us of the Father's highest blessings and his will for us.

Fellowship with the Father has, as a result, very practical implications. The Christian, as he hears the Father speak in ways in which he has already spoken through his Word, sees and understands again how he should live. The mandates and the will of God become clearer. The Christian thereby acquires new insights, new confirmations of the directions he should take, confirming convictions of God-glorifying courses in life, and the "peace that passes understanding" (Phil 4:7) that comes with the assurance that he lives within the will of his Father.

What is to be said more expansively of fellowship with the Father becomes clear to the Christian experientially as he comes to the Father in faith and true worship. He knows, with gradual and opening wideness, the meaning of his Father's love and purposes for him. He knows more clearly the "joy unspeakable and full of glory" (1 Pet 1:8) that comes from knowing God in his Son Jesus Christ. He knows, with a calmness born of worshipful communion with the Father, what at last is meant by the remarkable redemption and reconciliation with himself that God has provided. In such ways, the experience of fellowship with God teaches its own innermost meaning.

The benefits of the Christian's fellowship with the Father include its transforming effects. The relationship has a transforming effect in that it enables the believer to say with Paul in his letter to the Galatians, "I live; yet not I, but Christ liveth in me; and the life which I now live in the flesh I live by the faith of the Son of God, who loved me, and gave himself for me" (Gal 2:20). It is transforming in that God has made the Christian a "partaker of the divine nature" (2 Pet 1:4). By that it is meant, not that the Christian is absorbed into the essence of God. We observed previously that Christian regeneration does not involve the divinization of man. But the Christian is made a partaker of the divine nature in that the Holy Spirit endows him progressively with the communicable attributes of God. He does that to the extent and in the degree that the Christian believer is being prepared for the place he has been ordained to occupy in the eternal kingdom of glory.

On the grounds of his fellowship with God, though, as we shall see, the Christian's experiential awareness of the high privilege of that fellowship may falter, the Christian can know with unsullied assurance that his heavenly Father knows all about him and waits to hear his worship and praise and to hear his needs and petitions. He knows that his Father is his sure retreat in every storm, a rescue from the gales and cares of his life. But more than that, the Christian knows by virtue of his innermost conviction and awareness of it, that his Father has declared his love for him, an everlasting love, born of divine will from all eternity, that will never fail nor change. The Christian knows, with an assurance that the gates of hell cannot destroy though they may attempt to shake it, that the Father has again and again given to him the testimony of the Holy Spirit that he is, in truth, a child of his heavenly Father, destined to eternal joy in his very presence.

The Ground of Fellowship with the Father

What is it, then, in which fellowship with the Father, or, indeed, the very possibility of that fellowship, is grounded? John gives us the answer in the seventh verse of his first chapter. It is the fact that "the blood of Jesus Christ his [God's] Son cleanseth us from all sin." Now it is useful at this point to observe two respects in which it is possible to misread the apostle's intention at that important point.

First, John has raised in the preceding verses (to which we shall return) the distinction between two classes of people, the understanding of which is to be held carefully as John's epistle proceeds. One class of people "walk in the light" as God is in the light, and the other class continue to "walk in darkness." That dichotomy, or that division between two clearly definable classes of people, comes into focus repeatedly throughout John's epistle. Every individual is in one class or the other. With that in view, John then says that "if we walk in the light, as he [God] is in the light, we have fellowship one with another" (1 John 1:7). Now that "one with another" is not to be taken to refer to the fellowship that does, or should, exist between

The Christian's Highest Good

fellow members of the church, though John will insist at later points of his letter on the importance of a fellowship of mutual love among the saints of God. At this beginning point of his letter the reference is to the fellowship that exists between God the Father and the Christian person. The "one with another" refers to the Christian and his heavenly Father.

The second possible misreading of this seventh verse of John's first chapter takes us to the heart and essence of his principal concern and thesis. Let us put the point negatively. The verse does not have reference to the quality or consistency of the Christian's walk in this life. The text is that "if we walk in the light . . . we have fellowship." It might appear on the surface of things that John is making a statement there about the condition on the grounds of which we have fellowship with the Father; in the sense that if we walk in the light we have fellowship, and if, for some reason, we cease to walk in the light we do not have fellowship. If that were the sense of the verse it would be speaking to the quality of the Christian's walk in the faith that he professes. But the apostle's statement is to be understood on a very different level. To see what is involved, we must refer again to the underlying statement in the verse that "the blood of Jesus Christ cleanseth us from all sin."

John is not addressing at this point the fact that if and when we sin in our Christian walk, the blood of Christ cleanses us. We shall see later in his first chapter the important sense in which, of course, that cleansing does occur. If that was in view at this initial point, this opening statement of John would have to be seen as having reference to what occurs in the life of the Christian believer in the progress of his sanctification. But for reasons of the manner in which this epistle of John is structured, the reference to the blood of Jesus Christ here in verse 7 has reference, not to the Christian's sanctification, but to his justification. John will address what is, in effect, the question of the Christian's progress in sanctification in subsequent verses in his first chapter.

The epistle's concern at this initial point with the "blood of Jesus Christ" as providing the ground of the Christian's justification is to be recognized in a very important sense. For when John introduced his letter by stating that the Christian's highest good is fellowship with the Father, it was necessary to state, beyond that, what it is on which that fellowship is grounded. And he is saying at this point that the fellowship is grounded in the fact of the redemptive work of the Lord Jesus Christ. That substitutionary life and death of Christ provides the grounding of the very possibility of fellowship with God. Again, it is because God has set forth in his Son a propitiation for sin, as John will address that later in his letter beginning with the second chapter, that the possibility of fellowship with God and with his Son Jesus Christ exists.

The first two of our questions in this chapter have been answered by the apostle: first, it is with God who is light, who is "in the light" (1 John 1:7), and who is the holy eternal God, with whom the fellowship of which we are speaking exists; second, the ground on which that fellowship has become possible is "the blood of Jesus Christ." We pause at this point to observe what is to be understood more precisely by what John has referred to as "the blood of Jesus Christ." The term clearly refers to, and takes up in its meaning, the full scope of the atonement that Christ offered for sin. As we have explored more fully in chapter two, when Christ died in his human nature he suffered in human soul and body. In agony of soul he passed through the pains of eternal hell and eternal death, and after returning triumphantly from that suffering of soul he laid down his life in temporal death, having committed his human soul to the Father. "The blood of Jesus Christ" in John's formula here is, then, an abbreviated reference to all that our Lord suffered, the incomprehensible extent of which provides the ground of our reconciliation with the Father. As the apostle Paul made the point in his letter to the Ephesians, it is "Through him [Christ] we have access by one Spirit unto the Father" (Eph 2:18).

Two Classes of People

The Christian's highest good, as the blessing of it accrues to him in this life, is fellowship with the Father and with his Son Jesus Christ. We have looked at that from several perspectives and considered the ground of it in the substitutionary death of Christ. We can now look more closely at several further implications of that highest good as John continues to address it in his First Epistle.

First, it must now be seen, as it applies to all that is to be said about the Christian status and life, that there are only two classes of people in the world. There are the regenerate on the one hand and the unregenerate on the other. Abraham Kuyper, a prominent theologian-statesman in the Netherlands in the late nineteenth century, has made the point in a particularly interesting way. He speaks at length of what he refers to as "Two Kinds of People," explaining the respects in which God's work of regeneration in the soul establishes the difference between them. Kuyper refers repeatedly to what he means by the word "palingenesis," the transliteration of the underlying Greek word meaning regeneration, or being born again. "We speak none too emphatically, therefore," Kuyper observes, "when we speak of two kinds of people. Both are human, but one is inwardly different from the other, and consequently feels a different content rising from his consciousness; thus they face the cosmos from different points of view, and are impelled by different impulses." In an apologetic essay whose detail cannot detain us at this point, Kuyper observes further that because of the differentiation he has already established there are "Two Kinds of Science."[3]

But the doctrinal concept on which Kuyper has insisted is substantiated by the scriptural data that guides our discussion. The apostle Paul, in the context of his detailed scrutiny of the character of the natural man in sin, has made the point in the first chapter of his letter to the Romans. There are, he says, covenant-keepers and there are covenant-breakers (Rom 1:31). That casts our minds back to the original status in which man was established as he came from the hands of his Creator. Man, in short, is a covenant creature. And notwithstanding our first parent's fall and his repudiation of his obligations under the covenant of creation (also referred to as the covenant of works or the covenant of life), all those descending from him by ordinary generation, all of his natural posterity, remain under obligation to the requirements of that original covenant. That relationship derives from the fact that Adam was established by his Creator as the federal head and representative of all who would by natural means descend from him. Adam was thus a public person.

That highly significant distinction between classes of people is stated in John's first epistle in a particularly informative way. In making that twofold classification, John identifies the respective members of the classes as follows. On the one hand, he says, there are those who "walk in the light," and there are others who "walk in darkness." That dichotomy is basic and fundamental to everything that is to be said of the Christian from that point on. As to the identification of those in the first class, those who "walk in the light," their status depends entirely on the grace of God who, by the regenerating work of his Holy Spirit within them, has brought them to see the reconciliation with him that Christ has provided. They are his elect people. They are the ones who are "called according to his purpose" (Rom 8:28).

Those persons who are now identified as the ones who "walk in the light" are who and what they are because, as Paul again states it in his letter

---

3. Kuyper, *Principles*, 152–55.

The Christian's Highest Good

to the Colossians, they have been "delivered from the power of darkness and translated into the kingdom of his [God's] dear Son" (Col 1:13). A definitive transference has taken place. Once, those people were "ungodly," because they had not kept the law of God. But now they have been regarded as "godly," by reason of the imputation to them of the righteousness of Christ who kept the law on their behalf. They have turned from their idols to Christ (1 Thess 1:9), in conscious and whole-souled exercise of the saving faith that was conveyed to them by the Spirit of God. That being given, when John now refers to those who "walk in the light" he is not, in the first place, making any reference to the quality of that walk, or the quality of the Christian life that one may or may not exhibit. On the contrary, if we are to grasp the meaning of the Christian's highest good at this critical point, we have to see that John is speaking not of the quality of life but of a designated status in which the Christian person stands and exists. He is speaking, that is, about a particular class of people, and he will go on to speak at length of what characterizes them by virtue of their being "in the light." The most essential way to refer to or describe them is by that fundamental designation. Unlike other people, they are no longer "in the darkness."

John goes on to make a profoundly true statement that influences again the structure of his letter from that point on. In the sixth verse of his first chapter he makes a very pointed reference to those who, unlike the persons we have just described, are still "walking in darkness." As he will explicitly refer to some of them again in the nineteenth verse of his second chapter, there are some who, while they are still numbered among those who "walk in darkness," nevertheless make the false claim that they do, in fact, have "fellowship with God." "No," John says vehemently. If such people make that kind of claim, their claim is demonstrably false, and they "lie, and do not the truth" (1 John 1:6). Only the first class of people can say that they possess that highest good of fellowship with God. The false claims of the rest identify them as liars. John's language is abrupt and severe.

Lloyd-Jones has grasped the distinction we have now made, and he has remarked at length on its importance for understanding the Christian's true status. "When we come to this verse about 'walking in the light', we interpret it as just the antithesis and the exact opposite of 'walking in darkness'. . . . It mean[s] that I claim that I belong to a different realm, to the kingdom of light and to the kingdom of God. In that kingdom, alas, I may be most unworthy; but though unworthy, I am in it and I belong to it and I am walking in the realm of light. . . . Every Christian of necessity is one who is walking in the light. The non-Christian is the one who is walking in darkness"[4]

The second thing to be said about the Christian's highest good is that the fellowship about which John is speaking is not something the Christian believer is to work towards and finally reach and realize. What is involved is not some higher aspect of Christian character and privilege that may, after sufficient endeavor and struggle, come into one's grasp and enjoyment. To the contrary, fellowship with the Father is the high privilege and status of every new-born Christian by reason of the very fact that he is a Christian. For what establishes that new status is the fact that such a person has been made regenerate by the grace of God. Now, by reason that he thereby is made a son of God, born with a nature that reflects that of his heavenly Father, a son of God by birth, all of the privileges consequent on his new status belong to him. They belong to him by God's redemptive design and eternal decree. They are his immediately, and it is open to him to enjoy them to the full as his walk with Christ proceeds and matures.

We shall go on to see that a vastly important distinction is to be drawn between the Christian's new status and privileges as such and the extent to which certain other aspects of the Christian life call for examination. Two other things are to be said. First, the extent to which the new-born Christian is aware of the status of fellowship that now belongs to him, and the degree to which he particularizes it in his experience, will necessarily vary. Second, the extent to which, in his actual walk in the Christian life, he cultivates and lives consistently with the status of privilege that is actually his will also vary. It is important, at many stages of Christian doctrine, to distinguish the *objective facts* of the blessings that God has reserved for, and granted to, his people from their *subjective realization* and enjoyment of those blessings. The possible confusion by the Christian on that important difference is undoubtedly the cause of weakness and ineffectiveness in the Christian life.

On such grounds it is true also that by reason of the imperfect development in holiness of the faculties of soul, sin inevitably continues in the experiential Christian life. That is true, even though when the Christian falls into occasions of sin he is no longer under the dominion of sin. For his existential status has been dramatically changed. The apostle Paul has stated it clearly in his letter to the Romans: "Our old man is crucified with Christ, that the body of sin might be destroyed, that henceforth we should

---

4. Lloyd-Jones, *Fellowship with God*, 127–28.

not serve sin. . . . Reckon ye also yourselves to be dead indeed unto sin, but alive unto God through Jesus Christ our Lord. . . . Sin shall not have dominion over you" (Rom 6:6, 11, 14).

The high status, then, of fellowship with God is the property of every Christian, it is his at the very beginning of his Christian life and experience, and by reason of its grounding in the redemptive design of God it is indestructible.

The Christian's Sin

The Christian person no longer lives in the realm of darkness. He is no longer "walking in darkness." The transformation of life and status due to the renewing grace of God has taken place. He is now "walking in the light." But an important distinction remains to be drawn between that new existential status as such and the experiential life of the Christian in the world. In short, we must realize the all too serious danger, and we must take account of the all too clear reality, of sin in the life of the Christian. Though he is now a truly regenerate person, and though he has been raised to the new high status of union with Christ and fellowship with the triune Persons of the Godhead, nevertheless he sins.

As we consider now the apostle's discussion of the life of such a person, we are speaking of sin in the life of those who are in fellowship with God. We observe two things about them: First, the fact of their sin does not mean that they are no longer "walking in the light." If that statement in itself appears to contain a contradiction, that arises, we have to say, from a serious failure to grasp adequately what the apostle is teaching in his epistle and what is the substance of the apostolic doctrine as we have already observed it at these points. Lloyd-Jones has observed on that important point in drawing our attention again to the very definition and existential status of the Christian. "The Christian is not a man or woman who ought to be walking in the light but who so often is walking in darkness. The Christian is one who, by definition here, is always walking in the light even though he falls into sin. By falling into sin you do not return to walking in darkness. The Christian is not a Christian at all unless he is walking in the light. . . . Christians do not spend their lives walking in and out of the kingdom of God; we are all by nature in the kingdom of darkness, and by becoming Christians we are translated, put into, the kingdom of God. . . . It is a daring statement in a sense, yet it is scriptural: if I fall into sin I am still in

The Christian's Highest Good

the kingdom of God. I am not walking in darkness because I have sinned; I am still in the realm of light."[5] The meaning of what is said is that two distinct and separate realms exist. One is the realm of light, and the other is the realm of darkness. The Christian is a person who has been definitively transformed from the latter to the former. Whatever is to be said of him from that point on is to be said of a person who is for ever in the realm of light. That means that he is one who is "walking in the light."

We can make the point in a different way. We have seen that the Christian's highest good is fellowship with the Father and with his Son Jesus Christ. When the Christian sins, that does not mean that his fellowship with God has been destroyed. Sin tarnishes that fellowship and it grieves the Holy Spirit who ministers the grace of God to us as we walk in the Christian life, but on confession of sin God will cleanse the one who is his child of all unrighteousness.

Second, the relation we have just acknowledged can be examined further in the light of what is to be said of Christian personhood. The person who has been made regenerate by the Holy Spirit's work within the soul is now a new man, "the old man has been crucified with Christ" (Rom 6:6), and "old things are passed away, all things are become new" (2 Cor 5:17). That newness of personhood involves the fact that there is not now in the regenerate person both an old nature and a new nature. There is abroad in the evangelical church, and even in evangelical scholarship at the present time, misunderstanding on the point. Some who claim that there is still within the Christian an "old nature" go on to say that when the Christian sins it is the old nature that is sinning. But it must be said that when the Christian sins, it is the Christian *person* who sins, and the person is responsible and accountable for his sin. The Christian person is to be described by, or characterized by, a new nature. The nature describes and defines the person. When, then, the Christian sins, he is sinning in his new nature, and it is that that grieves the Holy Spirit (Eph 4:30) and tarnishes the sweetness and joy of the Christian's fellowship with God. It is the fact that the Christian sins *in his new nature* that underlines the gravity of sin and the shame of it in the Christian life.

The biblical data present the antidote and remedy for sin. Reflecting the issues of status and life to which we have referred, Paul argues to the Colossian church: "As ye have therefore received Christ Jesus the Lord, so walk ye in him" (Col 2:6). And to the Galatians he says in similar vein: "If

---

5. Ibid., 142.

we live in the Spirit, let us also walk in the Spirit" (Gal 5:25). The ethical imperative is clear and need not be rehearsed at length to the practiced Christian. But what of the remedy for sin? "If we confess our sin," John states, "He [God] is faithful [that is, he is faithful and just in himself (Rom 3:26) and he is covenantally faithful to those whom he has redeemed] to forgive us our sin, and to cleanse us from all unrighteousness" (1 John 1:9). It is on that level, in that respect, and for that purpose that the Christian has the free and unimpeded access to the Father which unbroken and unbreakable fellowship with God provides to him. He has access to the very throne room of heaven as he comes in repentance and contrition. The Father, with unbounded love, waits to receive him again.

We do well to be alert to the deceitfulness of sin. Sin is hideous. It is treacherous and subtle, and the devil with his fallen angels who "kept not their first estate" (Jude 6), can be deceptively "transformed into an angel of light" (2 Cor 11:14). But what is sin, and how easily can the careless "walker in light" be deceived and fall into sin? If the Christian ignores his sin, and if, more damaging to the soundness of his "fellowship with God" and the joy it renders possible, he ignores the Holy Spirit's convicting his conscience of sin, he is, as John also says, deceiving himself and to that extent he is living a lie. The truth, at that point is "not in him" (1 John 1:8).

What, then, is sin? Sin, John tells us (1 John 3:4), is "the transgression of the law." In the context of the Christian's progress in sanctification, that reminds us that the moral law of God is the rule of life for the Christian believer. He is to know the law, to love the law, and to strain every nerve to live according to the law. Again, sin is whatever, in speech or action or social and cultural commitment, offends or outrages the holiness of God (recall 1 John 1:5). Sin is what turns the Christian's focus and orientation of life from God to himself. Sin may be active and deliberate, a forthright acting against a godly conscience, or it may be passive, a failure to do what should be done, an omission. What is involved may be sin of ignorance. That does not mean ignorance of the law. For compare David's prayer: "Cleanse thou me from *secret faults*" (Ps 19:12); or the words of Moses in Psalm 90:8, "Thou hast set our iniquities before thee, our *secret sins* in the light of thy countenance." The true believer may not even be conscious of sins that are for a time hidden from his awareness. How subtle sin and the danger of sin is! How we as God's people should be alert to that subtlety!

But what is the ground on which God can forgive the Christian's sin, can call him again to himself, make him again conscious of his covenantal privileges, and can restore him, not to fellowship with him, not to again "walking in the light," but to the joy and the contentment of the unbreakable fellowship with himself that his very being born again connoted? The ground on which God can forgive the sin is the fact that our Lord Jesus Christ has already paid the penalty for all our sin. When Christ died on our behalf he provided a complete and total atonement for all our sin, past, present and future. There could never, therefore, be any further condemnation (Rom 8:1), our "old man," the Adamic man, was "crucified with Christ" (Rom 6:6); he is dead and gone; and we have the clear mandate from God to "reckon ourselves to be dead indeed unto sin, but alive unto God" (Rom 6:11). The method by which God "cleanses us" when we have sinned is by the calming assurance of sonship that he conveys to us by his Holy Spirit. Because he has "loved us with an everlasting love" (Jer 31:3) he again draws us to himself, he confides his love to us, and he heals the broken heart of contrition that we bring to him.

But a terrible warning remains. If we continue to ignore our sin we not only lie in ourselves. We "make him [God] a liar" (1 John 1:10); that is, we reject his promise that he will forgive us and cleanse us. Further, if we were to respond to the subtle overtures of Satan and imagine that we could "continue in sin that grace may more abound" (Rom 6:1) we would fall into the trap of self-deception and antinomianism. The more the reason, then, why we should be diligent in prayer that God will preserve in us a conscience that is acutely sensitive to the danger and meaning of sin that grieves him (Eph 4:30).

In the ways we have now examined, the Christian's highest good exists in the privilege that is accorded him of "fellowship with the Father and with his Son Jesus Christ." In the light of that, there lies ahead the need to reflect on the essential characteristics exhibited by those who, by the grace of God, have been admitted to that status. Before we turn to consider some of the issues that are relevant on that level, however, it will be useful to reflect in the following chapter on one further aspect of the redemptive activity of our Lord that has made all of those privileges and blessings possible. We shall look in relatively brief terms at the propitiatory and intercessory activities of Christ as important aspects of his discharge of his high priestly office. For it is those actions that both make the Christian believer's privileges possible and which guarantee the communication of them to him.

five

The Propitiation and Intercession of Christ

The Christian's highest good is grounded in the finished sacrificial work in this world of the Second Person of the Godhead. Fulfilling his covenantal commitment in the execution of his redemptive office that was declared in the council of the Godhead before the foundation of the world, he came into the world to become Jesus Christ and, in impeccable obedience, to fulfill the will of the Father. That will and purpose was that sinners whom he had chosen to share his eternal glory with him should be reconciled to himself.

We have observed in an earlier chapter that the divine intent in Christ's coming is spanned by his destruction of the works of the devil (1 John 3:8; Heb 2:14), and by his provision for his people of what the apostle John referred to as life more abundantly (John 10:10). We shall not address in any full sense at this point the glory of Christ as he discharged his redemptive office. Relevant literature is readily available in the Reformed theological tradition. John Owen, in usual magisterial fashion, has addressed that expansively.[1] And more recent essays have supplemented Owen's great work.[2] Our purpose here is more modest. From the range of issues that warrant close attention and deserve meditation we shall make some mini-

---

1. See Owen, "The Person of Christ," *Works*, 1:1; "The Glory of Christ," *Works*, 1:274; "The Glory of Christ applied to Sinners and Saints," *Works*, 1:417.

2. See the valuable extensive treatment in Turretin, *Elenctic Theology*. Cunningham has addressed relevant issues insightfully in his *Historical Theology*, 237–70. For a recent collection of relevant essays see Beeke, *The Beauty and Glory of Christ*.

mal comments on two important questions. First, what is to be understood as the propitiation for sin that Christ offered in his substitutionary sacrifice; and second, to look again at the completion of his redemptive work, what is to be understood as the intercession he now makes for the people he redeemed as he conducts his heavenly high priestly office?

But an initial question presses and calls for at least minimal address: Who was it that paid on the cross the penalty for the sins of his people? It was the Son of God. And a careful understanding is required of who it was in his *person* who made that vital atoning sacrifice. We have said that in his offering of himself Christ died *in his human nature*. That is demonstrably true. But our present question requires the recognition that it was the *person* of Christ in that human nature who paid the price of sin. A larger exposition of the relevant doctrines would require a close examination of the Chalcedonian settlement on the doctrine of the Person of Christ.[3] He took a true and sinless human nature into union with his divine nature. And in that human nature he, the sinless Son of God, was made sin for us (2 Cor 5:21). He was not made a sinner. But God the Father "laid on him" (Isa 53:6) the sin of those for whom he died. He was made guilty, not of his own sin, for he had no sin, but of the sin of those whom the Father had given to him to redeem. The sin he bore was *extrinsic* to him. It was not, and by reason of his divine personhood and sinless human nature it could not have been, *intrinsic*. A close and extensive examination is accordingly required on the relation between the *Person* and the *work* of Christ.

William Cunningham has addressed that highly important relation and observes that "It is plain, from the nature of the case, that the subjects of the *person* and the *work* of Christ must be, in fact and in doctrine, intimately connected with each other."[4] A more expansive discussion is contained in the treatises of John Owen.[5] There was necessarily a communication of mind between the divine and human natures in Christ. But there was not a communication of properties between the two natures. We noted previously such errors as those of the Eutychians in the early church who argued that at the incarnation of our Lord the human nature was absorbed into the divine and that Jesus Christ was, therefore, to be regarded as one person in one nature. But it is to be held, to the contrary, that in our Lord the divine nature remained divine, without communication to it of

---

3. See the discussion in chapter 2.
4. Cunningham, *Historical Theology*, 2:238, italics added.
5. See note 1 above.

any properties of the human nature, and that in a corresponding respect the human nature remained purely human. Owen addresses the relevant complex of doctrines at length. Referring to the Person of Christ, he says that "the thing to be considered in his person [is] the communion or mutual communication of the distinct natures."[6] Owen understands, that is to say, that the two natures are, as he says, "distinct," but that while that was so, there was a communication of mind between them. That arose because, as we referred to the situation previously, the two natures of our Lord were such that by reason that he took unto himself a true and reasonable human soul there were in him both a divine mind and a human mind, both a divine and a human capacity for affection, and both a divine and a human will.

Owen drives home the necessary understanding that it was the *person* of Christ who offered himself for us in order to seal our salvation: "The *divine nature* knows all things, upholds all things, rules all things, acts by its presence everywhere; the *human nature* was born, yielded obedience, died, and rose again. *But it is the same person,* the same Christ, that acts all these things."[7] Owen confirms the doctrine by observing that "He [Christ] is the Lord of glory [1 Cor 2:8] on account of his divine nature only; thence is his *person* denominated when he is said to be crucified, which was in the human nature only."[8]

Propitiation

The doctrine of propitiation has been variously treated in the history of biblical translation and commentary. The principal points at issue warrant careful attention and can be summarized as follows.

First, the doctrine is stated in four contexts in the apostolic literature: in 1 John 2:2, 1 John 4:10, Romans 3:25, Hebrews 2:17. Each of these locations deserves close study and reflection. In the context of exhibiting the love of God John makes the defining statement: "He [God] loved us and sent his Son to be the propitiation for our sins" (1 John 4:10), and he adds that "he is the propitiation for our sins; and not for ours only, but also for the sins of the whole world" (1 John 2:2). We shall return to John's statements at those points.

---

6. Owen, *Works*, 1: 232.
7. Ibid., 234, italics added.
8. Ibid., 235, italics added.

The Christian's Highest Good

The word and the concept of "propitiation" means setting at peace. In the present case, by virtue of the substitutionary life and death of Christ, God the Father is set at peace. That is to say, the justice and wrath of God against sin has been appeased. For that reason it is stated at Romans 8:1 that "There is therefore now no condemnation"; and at Romans 5:1, that "We have peace with God." It is important to contrast Romans 5:1 with Philippians 4:7. The import of the former is that because of the propitiation that Christ effected, God is at peace with us. Philippians 4:7, on the other hand refers to the subjective "peace that passes understanding" which the Christian enjoys by virtue of the ministry of God to him. It is because God the Father has taken the initiative in dealing with our sin in the Person of his Son that the high privileges of which we have spoken do, in fact, belong to the Christian person. Those privileges are interminably, indestructibly, indissolubly his. They belong to him by sovereign divine grant.

Second, it should be noted carefully that the text at this point says that *Christ* is the propitiation for our sins. That is, it is Christ himself who is the propitiation, or who is the propitiator. He is the propitiation in and by virtue of the redemptive work he has done. We hold carefully to the fact, similarly, that it is Christ himself who has saved us. He has done that by, and in, the work he has completed on our behalf. But we recognize, and we hold the fact carefully in our understanding of our redemption, that it is Christ himself who is the object of our saving faith. Christ was both the priest who made the offering and was himself the offering. He himself was "the Lamb of God, which taketh away the sin of the world" (John 1:29).

Third, some translations of the Scriptures avoid the use of the word "propitiation" in this (1 John 4:10) and comparable contexts. For example, the New International Version employs the phrase "atoning sacrifice," and other translations use the word "expiation" in place of "propitiation." Such variations in translation are no doubt associated with the fact that the doctrine of the wrath of God, which, as has been shown, is vitally involved in the fact of propitiation, is uncongenial to some theologians. It is not universally understood and agreed, that is, that God is a God of wrath against sin, and that the reality of the wrath of God does not in any sense contradict or stand against the love of God. The wrath and the love of God are coordinate with his eternal holiness and the justice.

Was Christ, then, as the New International Version says, an atoning sacrifice for sin? Of course he was. To argue to the contrary would negate the very purpose of his coming into the world. Was he, as we shall observe again in a moment, the expiation for our guilt? Of course he was. Again, to argue to the contrary would destroy the very reason why he went willingly to the cross. But Jesus Christ, who bore the penalty of our sin on the cross, who suffered for us not only in human body but in human soul, was more than an atoning sacrifice for sin or the expiation for our guilt. He was the propitiation for our sin. The eternally holy God, whose holiness, justice, and righteousness had been outraged by our sin, who hates evil, who looks on sin not with complacence but with the wrath of displacement, must be satisfied. His wrath against sin must be set at peace. To argue to the contrary would not only negate the reason for Christ's appearance among men, but it would strike the death blow to the very revelation that God has made of his own being and holy purposes. If Christ were not the propitiation for our sin, not only would the character and consistency of God be impugned, but the heart would be torn from what he has revealed of his covenantal objective of redemption. The very meaning of his own covenantal faithfulness would be destroyed.

Fourth, an important difference of meaning exists in the words "propitiation" and "expiation." Expiation means the erasure of guilt. Of course, in his death Christ was both the expiation and the propitiation for our sins. By the former it is meant that the guilt of our sins was completely dealt with, so that whereas we were, before our expression of saving faith in Christ, "guilty" and "ungodly," now, by his death and the imputation of his righteousness to us we are accounted in the counsel of God as guiltless and godly. In short, propitiation is addressed to God's justice and wrath, and expiation is addressed to the sinner's guilt. It bears repetition that the righteousness of Christ is imputed to us in such a way that God the Father now looks on us as though we have not sinned. And moreover, because Christ has paid a complete and perfect penalty for our sins God looks on us as though we had, in fact, paid that penalty ourselves. But the distinction in the very meaning of words requires it to be said that in the substitutionary sacrifice of Christ, not only was our guilt removed, but, of profoundly significant moment, the wrath of God was appeased.

Fifth, when Christ is said in 1 John 2:2 to be the propitiation for the sins "of the whole world," that does not mean that his atonement was a universal atonement, or that in his death he bore the guilt of the sins of all people. We do not see in that statement any endorsement of the theological doctrine of universalism in salvation. Universalism with respect to Christ's atonement is the province of Karl Barth, the early twentieth-century neo-orthodox theologian, and the Arminians. We do not hold to a general or indiscriminate atonement. To do so would be to endorse the claims of Arminianism, whose revival of the Pelagian theory of human autosoterism we looked at previously. Such a mistaken doctrine of universalism would also find hospitality in the teaching of Amyraldianism that emerged, following the Reformation, as a failed attempt to establish a mediating theology between the Reformed theology and that of the Arminians. The Scriptures teach a particular atonement, and their declaration is clear that in his atonement Christ actually saved his people. He did not die merely to make salvation possible.

While that is so, we hold to an indiscriminate offer of the gospel, declaring the invitation of Christ that whosoever will may come to him and "take of the water of life freely" (Rev 22:17). That invitation is spread liberally across the pages of Scripture and will be familiar. When it is said, in the preaching of the gospel that "whosoever will" may come, the question may arise in some minds as to why anyone would not come. Or again, it may be asked, who will come? The answer, of course, as the biblical doctrine is expansive in stating, is that only those will come whom the Holy Spirit arrests, to whom he grants his secret, sovereign, and unsolicited grace of regeneration. Then those who are the beneficiaries of that work will come freely, their minds and hearts and wills having been renewed with the capacities, abilities, and the free dispositions to do so.

Sixth, when it is said in 1 John 2:2 that Christ is the propitiation for the sins of the whole world, the focus of thought does not fall on the extent of the atonement. What the apostle is placing before us at that point is not the question of who it was for whom Christ died. He is concerned, not with the extent of the atonement or the identity of those who were the beneficiaries of it, but with the identity of the one who made the atonement. He is interested at that point in the identity of the propitiator. He is insisting, that is, that there is only one propitiator, Jesus Christ. And wherever sins are propitiated, anywhere in the world, they are propitiated by that one propitiator, the Lord Jesus Christ whom the Father sent into the world to redeem those whom he had given to his Son for that purpose. Jesus Christ alone is competent to be our propitiator because he alone is the truly righteous one. As the hymn writer has put it, "There was no other good enough to pay the price of sin; / he only could unlock the gate of heav'n, and let us in."[9]

---

9. Alexander, "There is a Green Hill Far Away." In *Trinity Hymnal*, 256.

It should be noted that at 1 John 4:10, for example, the apostle sets the doctrine of propitiation in the context of the love of God. To understand the meaning of love, John says, it is necessary to look, not in the first place at any state of human conceptions or emotions, but at the way in which God has demonstrated his love for us. That was demonstrated in God's sending his Son to be the sacrificial substitute for the sinners. The purpose was that they "might live through him" (1 John 4:9), that they who were "dead in trespasses and sins" (Eph 2:1) might be raised to newness of life. John is glorying in the demonstrated love of God.

Is it possible, we may ask, to measure the vastness of that love? Let us recall the statement of John at the very beginning of his epistle. God, he states, is a holy God. "God is light, and in him is no darkness at all" (1 John 1:5). If, then, we want to conceive of the vastness of God's love, we could measure it if we could measure the distance God's Son came from that eternal light and holiness to die in humiliation for our sin. Or to put it differently, if we could measure that distance it would begin to give us some understanding of the depth and extent of the true meaning of sin, of the sinful heinousness of sin that an old Puritan writer called "the plague of plagues,"[10] for which Christ came to atone. If we could measure the complete unworthiness of the state in which, as the fallen children of Adam, we stood in the sight of God, we could begin to measure the extent and magnitude of his love. But these things are beyond us. The sinfulness of our sin is beyond measure. And the love of God is beyond measure. We therefore bow in worship before the eternal God who, by setting his love upon us to the immeasurable extent of sending his Son to bear the penalty for sin and reconcile us to himself, has admitted us, unworthy sinners though we are, to fellowship with him. That privilege of fellowship with him, we have said, is the Christian's highest good.

Intercession

Christ's discharge of his high priestly office is not exhausted by what we have recalled as his substitutionary, sacrificial offering for sin and the propitiation he offered to the Father. "Christ executes the office of a priest," the Westminster Shorter Catechism tells us, "in his once offering up of himself a sacrifice to satisfy divine justice, and reconcile us to God, and in making

---

10. Venning, *The Plague of Plagues*.

continual intercession for us."[11] The heavenly intercessory office of Christ has highly important significance for what we are referring to as the Christian's highest good.

We have observed at several points that at the instant of his regeneration by the sovereign will and grace of God, and by the conveyance of that grace to him by the secret, sovereign, and unsolicited act of the Holy Spirit, the person who is the beneficiary of that grace is joined to Christ in a vital and indissoluble union. Moreover, that union carries with it union with the three Persons of the Godhead. Clearly, from that point on, God in his triune Personhood does not leave his new-born child to himself. Those who have been brought to faith in Christ are now the sons of God, made sons by their new birth, born with the nature of God. For that reason, the active relation to that new-born son of the triune God, of each of the Persons of the divine Trinity in their distinguishable personhoods, discloses the redemptive love of God. In all of the acts of God external to the Godhead, in his works of creation, providence, and redemption, each of the three Persons is engaged. In that way, each of the three Persons of the Godhead is vitally and actively engaged in bringing the sons of God to glory. The divine relations involved in that could be expanded at length. But something of what is involved can be suggested in the following comments, as we consider briefly the joint operations of the divine Persons.

Christ, having passed into the heavens and having "an unchangeable priesthood . . . is able also to save them to the uttermost that come unto God by him, seeing that he ever liveth to make intercession for them" (Heb 7:25). It is clearly declared that "we have not an high priest which cannot be touched with the feeling of our infirmities, but was in all points tempted like as we are, yet without sin . . . [and we can therefore] come boldly unto the throne of grace, that we may obtain mercy, and find grace to help in time of need" (Heb 4:15–16). Such is the care of the triune God for his saints. Moreover, in that same context of divine interest and care, "Likewise the Spirit itself maketh intercession for us with groaning which cannot be uttered . . . because he maketh intercession for the saints according to the will of God" (Rom 8:26–27); and "It is Christ . . . who is even at the right hand of God who also maketh intercession for us" (Rom 8:34). So that in the same way as it has been said that the three Persons of the Godhead are engaged in all of the actions of God leading to and accomplishing our redemption, so here, in the important matter of the interests of the saints in

---

11. Westminster Shorter Catechism, Question 25.

The Propitiation and Intercession of Christ

their daily walk in this world and in the intercession for them, we are to see again the three Persons engaged. Christ himself intercedes for us with the Father, the Holy Spirit adds his intercession, and all is done in order that the will of God for us will be realized.

The fact that God in that way conveys to the Christian the assurance that Christ intercedes for him takes its place in the Christian mind as confirming and substantiating all that has been conveyed to him as his highest good. What, then, is to be said of the intercession that Christ conducts on the Christian's behalf? We have it stated that "if any man sin, we have an advocate with the Father, Jesus Christ the righteous" (1 John 2:1). The advocacy of Christ confirms the Christian's right of entry to the Father, and the following are some headings under which that divine activity on the Christian's behalf might be more fully discussed.

First, as he is now in heaven seated in authority at the right hand of the Father, Christ sees us as the "travail of his soul" (Isa 53:11). He looks on us as those he redeemed, and he takes pleasure in us. That is the height of the worth he has bestowed upon us. He takes satisfaction in contemplating us as he presents us to the Father. In doing that, he does not plead with or constrain the Father to love us. That is because the Father loved us before the foundation of the world, and it was on the ground of his eternal love that he "sent his Son to be the propitiation for our sins" (1 John 4:10). We acknowledge the mystery of the intercommunication between the Persons of the Godhead, and we bow before the mystery of the distinguishable personhood of the eternal Son and the Holy Spirit. We have said that the Spirit and the Son are autotheotic, that they are God in their own right from all eternity. We have spoken at length of the eternal generation of the Son by and from the Father, and the procession of the Holy Spirit from the Father and the Son.[12] Now, in again that divine communication, God the Son, our redeemer, presents us to the Father. He tells the Father of our state and condition in this world and he tells him of our sin.

Second, if we sin, Christ does not ask the Father to overlook our sin, or to let it be assumed for the moment that we have not sinned. If that were done it would violate the very integrity of God. It would not only be contrary to the eternal righteousness of God, but it would negate the very purpose of Christ's coming into the world and going to the cross for our redemption. It would negate the meaning of the Christian believer's true

---

12. See the appendix, "because Jesus was not yet glorified," in Vickers, *Discovering the Christian Mind*, 149–78.

The Christian's Highest Good

existential condition in the world as he is himself all too conscious that the residue of sin remains within him. That, however, does not contradict the reality that he is the "new creature" in Christ that his regeneration connotes, that he has in definitive fact been translated from the kingdom of darkness to the kingdom of God's dear Son (Col 1:13), that for him now "all things are new" (2 Cor 5:17). But as we have already seen, by reason of the imperfect development of the faculties of the soul in holiness and righteousness, the capacity to sin remains, and the Christian does as a result fall into occasions of sin, even though he has been rescued from the dominion of sin. That reality is at the heart of our entire argument that the Christian has not only been rescued from the tyranny of sin but has been raised to the immeasurable height and privilege of fellowship with the Father.

Third, Christ as our advocate does not ask the Father to make any change in the aspect in which he does then, or will from that time on, regard us. God is "the same yesterday, and today, and for ever" (Heb 13:8). To suggest that our sin would make any change in God's purpose and intention for us would not only negate what God has revealed to us as his eternal immutability, but it would destroy the reality of his operative care for us as a covenant-keeping God. When God made his covenant with Abraham he made the threefold promise that he would inherit a land, that he would be the father of many nations, and that God would be God to his people (Gen 17:4 8). The first two of those promises point to the church that Christ would build, such that "the gates of hell shall not prevail against it" (Matt 16:18), and to the eternal inheritance that God has reserved for the church. The fulfillment of the promises in Christ is spelled out in the apostolic statement that "if ye be Christ's, then are ye Abraham's seed, and heirs according to the promise" (Gal 3:29). As to the third of the promises, that God would be God to his people, the history of the entire process of redemption establishes God's faithfulness and veracity. In the instance now before us, when we say that Christ, in his intercessory activity, does not ask the Father to make any change in the aspect in which he regards us, that points again to the Father's covenantal faithfulness. In honoring his covenant he will never leave us or forsake us.

The intercession of Christ, therefore, does not, and in the very nature of God's purpose for his people it could not, contain any suggestion that God the Father should in any sense be asked to change his attitude toward us because of our sin. While that is so, that statement of what is at issue in God's covenantal arrangements and relations to his people does

The Propitiation and Intercession of Christ

not contradict or eliminate the fact that our heavenly Father is grieved by our sin. In short, we remember again that our whole condition as God's people is what it is because God has "loved us with an everlasting love," and because of that he has "drawn us" to himself (Jer 31:3). The simple statement that has been a relief to many troubled souls is apposite: "God has not loved us for our worthiness; and he will not forsake us because of our unworthiness."

Fourth, Christ presents our case to the Father as our advocate by saying to him that we are the people whom the Father gave to him to redeem (John 17:6, 9), that he has died for us and has paid all the penalty due to us for our sin, and that we are the ones he has assumed into union with himself. We should be conscious of the truth that in his death Christ definitively saved his people. He did not die simply to make their salvation possible. We do not hold, with Arminian theologians, a mere possibility theory of salvation. We do not hold to a theology that says that Christ has done all that he has, and all that could be done, to provide salvation for all mankind, and that it is now the sovereign responsibility of man to decide whether he will or will not accept the offer of salvation that Christ in his atonement made possible. If such were the case, man would have robbed God of his sovereignty and man himself would be sovereign.

That being so, when Christ presents his church to the Father, and when he intercedes with the Father on behalf of his people, individually and particularly, the Father joins with the Son in taking pleasure in the redeemed host that Christ has presented to him. If we were to imagine that the Christian's sin, notwithstanding the grief it brings to the Spirit of God in his sensitive care for us, breaks the existential bond of fellowship we have with the Father and the Son or, more expansively, with the triune God, we should be denying the very meaning of the death of God the Son in giving his life for our salvation.

Fifth, Christ, in that intratrinitarian communion that the Persons of the Godhead share, tells the Father in his advocacy for us that he, Christ, knows all about his people and their burdens and trials in their human nature, because he too suffered like things in *his* human nature. He tells the Father that he therefore sends his Holy Spirit to succor and comfort, and to heal in their brokenness the saints of God still in this world. He waits to receive them into the glorious eternal estate that he purchased for them. He sends his Holy Spirit to succor and comfort and guide his people in all of the difficulties they encounter and in their stumbling and their sins into which, for the moment, they fall. Christ says to the Father: "Thine they were, and thou gavest them me . . . I have given unto them the words which thou gavest me; and they have kept thy word" (John 17:6–8). The Christian's confidence therefore rests in the fact that the Father and the Son share the same covenantal commitment. "My Father which gave them me," Christ says, "is greater than all; and no man is able to pluck them out of my Father's hand" (John 10:29).

Sixth, at Christ's intercession and advocacy, our sin is not diminished or in any sense disguised. It is declared for what it is. But Christ says, in the satisfaction he realizes in the outcome of his mediatorial-redemptive accomplishment, that every aspect of the entailment of our sin has been dealt with, and our account with God has been settled for all eternity. The very fact that the Father has accepted the propitiation that Christ has provided, the fact that God is now at peace with his people, that he has declared that "there is therefore now no condemnation" (Rom 8:1), means that in actual fact "as far as the east is from the west, so far hath he removed [the condemnation of] our transgressions from us" (Ps 103:12). There is no falsity in the intercession of Christ as he presents us in our fallenness and sin to the Father. The relief from our faltering condition rests in the Father's assurance that "If we confess our sins, he is faithful and just to forgive us our sins, and to cleanse us from all unrighteousness" (1 John 1:9).

A second question asks why Jesus Christ, as he acts in the ways we have seen as our advocate with the Father, is referred to in the statement John has made as "righteous." John does not have principally in view at that point the intrinsic or essential righteousness that belongs to Christ by reason of his eternal identity as the Second Person of the Godhead. That in itself warrants our careful meditation and may not be completely absent from John's thought. Indeed, that may follow from the fact that at the ninth verse of his first chapter God is referred to as righteous or "just." And likewise, God the Son is righteous and just. But at issue now is the righteousness of Christ that he exhibited and fulfilled in the discharge of his messianic-mediatorial assignment. It was that righteousness, a righteousness under the law by virtue of his having fulfilled all the demands of the law, that qualified Christ to serve as our High Priest and now to intercede for us. It was because he was impeccably righteous, in all his forensic actions in this world as well as in his person, that the great exchange that sealed our salvation could be made. God, that is, imputed to Christ as our Substitute the guilt of our sin, and by reciprocal action he imputed to us the righteousness of Christ. We are saved eternally because God the Father has placed on us the perfect robe of righteousness of his Son (Isa 61:10). That having been done, when Christ as our advocate now presents us to the Father, the Father looks on us as though we had never sinned. Such is the completeness of the exchange that was involved in our redemption.

Conclusion

It is implicit in what we have said to this point that Christ's intercession for us is an integral part of his discharge of the responsibilities attaching to his high priestly office.[13] The fact that Christ, in his glorified state as the Second Person of the Godhead, should be presented to us as petitioning the Father on our behalf underlines his continual interest in us. That interest, it has now been seen, is extended in the execution of his priesthood to both the levels of providing the propitiation for our sin and his interceding in the courts of heaven for us. It would therefore be delinquent on our part to diminish either the propitiation or the intercession.

When he was in this world Christ expressed his jealousy for all those whom the Father had given to him to redeem. His high priestly prayer on their behalf, which he prayed in the hearing of his disciples on the night on which he was betrayed, speaks eloquently to that effect. His interceded then for them: "I pray for them," he said, "I pray not for the world, but for them which thou hast given me" (John 17:9). In his discourse on his identity as the good shepherd, as recorded in the tenth chapter of John's gospel, our Lord identified himself with his sheep, even to the point that he "called his own sheep by name" (John 10:3). When he died for them he knew the names of those whose sins he bore. He was "the good shepherd [who] giveth his life for the sheep" (John 10:11), and, he said, in projecting to them the security of his eternal design for them, "I give unto them eternal life, and they shall never perish, neither shall any man pluck them out of my hand" (John 10:28). Our Lord's heavenly intercession for his people, then, is to be seen as the projection into eternity of the love he had for them before time began, which brought him to die for them, and which guarantees their eternal rest and security in him.

---

13. For a very valuable discussion on relevant issues see Murray, "The Heavenly, Priestly Activity of Christ," in *Collected Writings*, 44–58.

six

Christian Distinctives

The argument that there are only two classes of people in the world turns on the results of the regenerating work of the Spirit of God in the hearts of his people. We adduced in that connection the claims of the apostle John in his First Epistle that one class is comprised of those people who are "walking in the light," while the other class of people are still "walking in darkness." Some are now in the realm of light. Others remain in the realm of darkness.

That differentiation lies at the root of the understanding of both the meaning of the Christian confession and the apologetic defense of it. The scriptural data on the point are copious. The implications of that class division extend to the walk of the Christian as he lives out his faith in the world. The still imperfect development in holiness of the faculties of soul causes him to fall into occasions of sin. But the incidence of the Christian's sin does not mean that he has thereby ceased to be "walking in the light." He is not in the kingdom of God at one time and fallen out of it at another. To the contrary, the significance of his sin, the shame of it and the torturous reality of it, is that it is the sin of one who, by the grace of God, is "walking in the light." When the Christian sins he is sinning in his new nature.

That differentiation extends its significance to the entire religious life of all people. By that we mean that by reason of his establishment as the image of God, which remains essential to the character of every man notwithstanding his participation in the fruits of Adam's fall, man as created is essentially and necessarily a religious being. He must worship. Either he will worship the true God from whose hands he has come, or he will worship a god constructed in his own imagination. He will worship an idol. In every man there is an ineradicable sense of God, the *sensus deitatis*, which, as Romans 1:18 states, is naturally suppressed when it rises unbidden to the level of consciousness, and a *semen religionis*, a seed of religion. Man will necessarily live, that is, according to the dictates of a *godly* religion, or by the imperatives of an *ungodly* religion.

The dichotomy that is thus clearly established in the Scriptures raises the question to which we now turn. If the Christian person is privileged to have been incorporated by God's redeeming grace into the class of people who are "walking in the light," what, then, do the Scriptures state as the characteristics that must necessarily describe him? In what respects are his knowledge capacities, his epistemic and ethical criteria, and his commitments and behavior patterns different from those of the world around him? By what necessary characteristics of life, that is, is he to be recognized and known?

Life in the World

To look again at John's epistle, he distinguishes between those who are "in the light" and those who are "in the darkness" in precise, even blunt, terms: "Love not the world," he says, "neither the things that are in the world. If any man love the world, the love of the Father is not in him. For all that is in the world, the lust of the flesh, and the lust of the eyes, and the pride of life, is not of the Father, but is of the world" (1 John 2:15–16). Against love of the Father, John sets the vastly different and conflicting love of the world. But what is "the world"? We reflect on several aspects before we look briefly at the apostle's immediate construction of it.

First, the world is fallen human nature that is fashioning human society in accordance with its own tendencies, the presuppositions and prescriptions of the "carnal mind" that is at "enmity against God . . . not subject to the law of God, neither indeed can be" (Rom 8:7). The world is the deliberate rejection of God. It, and life within it, is anthropocentric, centered on man for its attempted interpretation and search for meaning. It is the realm of intellectual, moral, and ethical autonomy against God. In his letter to the Ephesians Paul referred to the state of the Gentiles before the doors of the kingdom of God were thrown wide open to them. They were (i) without Christ, (ii) aliens from the commonwealth of Israel, (iii) strangers from the

Christian Distinctives

covenants of promise, (iv) having no hope, and (v) without God. And then, in order to summarize and drive home the meaning of all that as it applied to the Gentiles, he says that they were (vi) "in the world" (Eph 2:12). That is the strength of the indictment against all who are outside of Christ. They are "in the world," and the world is the realm in which God is deliberately shut out.

Further, "the world" from which the Christian is to be distinct conjures a cast of mind that is not only in fact, but with a conscious deliberateness, opposed to God. It will have nothing to do with God. God is excluded from all its thought-systems. As to the occupants of "the world," "There is no fear of God before their eyes" (Rom 3:18). Those who are still "in the world" live with the display of the reality of God and the display of his goodness before their eyes. But they have deliberately placed blinkers on their eyes so that they cannot see. Every man knows that God is, but man chooses to live outside of God. If any cognizance of God should be admitted, those "in the world" instinctively react by setting out to "prove" the existence of God on the grounds of the presupposition of the competence of unaided human reason. The competence of reason is the basic presupposition with which the task of explanation on all levels is approached.

That presupposition is characteristic of all forms of non-Christian reasoning in its attempts to explain states of affairs in the world and, to the extent that the question is engaged, the being of God and the possibility of relationship with him. It is necessary to say, also, that in some expressions of Christianity, at times in Reformed as well as in more widespread evangelical literature, the same underlying presupposition is held. But in a Christian apologetic, or in, that is, a rounded defense of the Christian faith, it is necessary to begin with a very different basic postulate. We begin with the declarative statement of Scripture that *God is* and that *he has spoken*. All that is, and all that eventuates, is what it is by virtue of the eternal dictates of the will of God. And, moreover, if a definitive "proof" of the existence of God is demanded, that proof exists in the sheer fact of the impossibility of the contrary. For if the explanation of all reality is not seen to be that which has been spoken into existence by the word of God, the only alternative that can be held is that all that is, and all that happens, comes to be and occurs by simple randomness and chance. But if that were so, there would then be no explanation of anything at all. There would be no reason why what happened did happen. Further, man himself would then be nothing other than a chance or random phenomenon. That would be the ultimate destruction of human personhood. Man would have no explanation of himself. Certainly it would be the blanket denial of human creaturehood. But by the unregenerate, non-Christian mind the necessary starting point that *God is* is deliberately rejected.

It follows also that the very atmosphere of love that informs the life of those who have "fellowship with the Father" is alien and completely unknown to those who are "in the world." "The things that are in the world," which should never claim the love of the Christian, are characterized by John as, first, the lust of the flesh. This phrase that John has used does not refer most immediately to things themselves that are the object of desire, but to the respects in which they are capable of having deleterious effects on the soul. Lust includes any inordinate desire or affection that displaces from the Christian mind the priority and the all-comprehending character of the love of God. To confine its meaning to the level of the physical, or the literal flesh, would diminish what is to be held in mind at this point. For anything, including those things which, in their proper place, might be legitimately glorifying to God, that absorbs the interest of the person to the displacement of the love of God and thereby becomes inordinate, is here condemned as contrary to the character of the "fellowship with the Father" of which John is speaking. In that sense, and addressing the danger for the Christian of inordinate desire for any thing, or entity, or person, or thought-system that takes the orientation of the Christian soul away from priority of love for God and the things of God, is to be brought under the condemnation of the lust of the flesh.

To make the statement in another way, anything that is taken to cater to the selfishness of personal pleasure, satisfaction, or imagined psychological fulfillment, to the extent that it is lusted after for its own sake independent of any possible God-glorifying aspect, is condemned in what the apostle has said. That is because what is in such a way lusted after, even though, if held in proper proportion, it may be legitimately glorifying to God, connotes a turning of the person and his affections on to himself and away from God. The Christian should be prepared to acknowledge that the lust that is here condemned may find expression even within the church and the activities and practices of the church. That can occur when activities that might be perfectly necessary in their proper place and engaged in for the glory of God, become matters of individual exhibitionism and detached from their sacred significance. The Savior's call to us for humility in our serving him clearly points in a very different direction.

Christian Distinctives

Second, John repudiates the "lust of the eyes." The eyes, of course, provide a gateway to the soul. In addition to what has just been said of the lust of the flesh, the apostle's statement here refers to all that engages the inordinate interest of the person because of its outward show, or because of its ability to cater to passions, and even actions that in themselves can lead to sin that is unworthy of the Christian. It includes the vanity of pomp and splendor, what appeals simply and only to the affective or emotional faculty of the soul and precipitates in the individual a love of mere impression. That applies to many things that the Christian is tempted to do and to agree with as they exist in the world and might be imported into the Christian's life. It may be clothing, the mere fad of fashion, or the exhibitionism of material things, or conformity to the mores of the world in various ways, in patterns of conduct, language, music, or entertainment for its own sake.

Third, John condemns and warns the Christian against "the pride of life." This is perhaps the most subtle of all. It can be summed up as self-glorification, inordinate ambition beyond the wish to please God by legitimate personal development, or the contempt of others in supposed climbing through social strata, pride of family, of name, or of social status, income, or anything that causes primary focus on the individual and not on the fact that he has a place in the kingdom of God. The pride of life can be expressed in a boasting of one's brain or imagined intelligence or developed gifts and skills, or of the school or college one attended. There are many dimensions on which absorption in the pride of life stands in stark antithesis against the love of God the Father.[1] But against all that, Christ has laid down the perfect direction for us: "Blessed are they that hunger and thirst after righteousness" (Matt 5:6).

But there is a further reason for not loving the world. "The world passeth away, and the lust thereof; but he that doeth the will of God abideth forever" (1 John 2:17). If one is foolishly, sadly, shortsightedly committed to the love of the world and the things in it rather than to the love of God, it can only be said of him that he will never find peace or fulfillment or satisfaction, and that he has been deluded into forgetting that his end is coming, the world is passing away, and the day of glory on the one hand and judgment on the other is soon to dawn. A reflection on such things projects one's thought from this present world to the eschatological terminus of all

---

1. See the valuable discussion of this question in Lloyd-Jones, *Walking with God*, 81–91. Our arguments throughout are indebted also to Candlish, *Commentary*.

things, to the great day of glory and judgment that is to appear. "Little children," John says, "it is the last time."

But before we leave this present subject, can it not be said that there is one respect in which we as God's people are to love the world? We are to love it as God loved it: "God so loved the world that he gave his only begotten Son, that whosoever believeth in him should not perish, but have everlasting life" (John 3:16). We can love the people in the world, darkened in sin and benighted as they are, by taking the good news of the gospel to them. We love them by showing them that the only way to reconciliation with God the Father, and thereby to fulfillment in life now and then life eternal and everlasting, is through Jesus Christ who "came into the world to save sinners" (1 Tim 1:15).

History laughs at the sinner. He imagines that the world provides him with the stability he seeks. But that is his highest and saddest fallacy. The world is passing away. History moves on the linear trajectory of divine intent. The day is coming, the great eschatological terminus, when "in the dispensation of the fullness of times [God will] gather together in one all things in Christ, both which are in heaven and which are on earth; even in him" (Eph 1:10). Then those who by the grace of God have learned the joys of the privilege of fellowship with God in this life will rise to the "inheritance . . . predestinated according to the purpose of him who worketh all things after the counsel of his own will" (Eph 1:11).

A final point is to be made: "He that doeth the will of God abideth for ever" (1 John 2:17). The statement implies not only that such a person can legitimately embrace the prospect of living for all eternity in the presence of God with whom he has fellowship in this life. That latter is beyond all doubt in prospect. But the "abideth for ever" in the text is saying that there is a priceless something that such a person has now that will abide, will continue for ever. For the reality of the Christian life and experience is that the fellowship with God that is now enjoyed in part will continue for all eternity in fuller state and more profound realization. That is well established by the apostle's statement that now, in this life, God has given to his people "the earnest," or the down payment, of what is to come in full measure in the eternal day (Eph 1:14). The Christian has now, at this very time as he progresses through the vale of tears in this world, an essential and indissoluble part of what he will receive in fullness in the age to come. That is what the person who is still "in the world," still "in darkness," knows, and can know, nothing about.

Christian Distinctives

Knowledge, History, and the Centrality of Christ

Those who do not live in fellowship with God but who live "in darkness" and not "in the light," do not understand that the world is "passing away" (1 John 2:17). They have no understanding of history as it is working out its way to the fulfillment of God's purpose. That purpose is directed not only to the redemption of God's chosen people, but to the dissolution of all things and the creation of "a new heaven and a new earth" (Rev 21:1). In doing so it is directed to the gathering together of all things in Christ (Eph 1:10). But on the contrary, those in fellowship with God do have a true sense and understanding of history. They know that "it is the last time" and that antichrists, certain forces in implacable opposition to God and his gospel, are abroad in the world. That has had significance for the history of the church, in that it has caused some false professors to be exposed for who and what they really are and they have therefore left the church (1 John 2:19).

At several points John has said that Christianity is a "we know" religion. For example, "*we know* that it is the last time" (1 John 1:18). By reason of a divine "unction," John says, "ye *know* all things" (1 John 1:20). And in the following verse, "ye *know* the truth." By reason of his having been raised to fellowship with God, the Christian has a perspective on both life and history, an intelligent understanding of God's purpose for the world, and a firm expectation of eternal life in the presence of God that is not available to men in this world.

The first thing being said here is that the Christian knows that he is living in the midst of a spiritual conflict. The text we have just referred to reminds us that in the last times "antichrist shall come." There is reason to believe that at that time the forces of evil will be personified in a certain individual, a "man of sin, the son of perdition" (2 Thess 2:3), "who opposeth and exalteth himself above all that is called God . . . so that he as God sitteth in the temple of God, showing himself that he is God" (2 Thess 2:4). But that ultimate personalization of evil is not the immediate concern at the point of John's context. The issue being confronted is concerned with the immediately contemporary condition, and with giving his readers, and thereby us in our own day, a preview of what we can expect to occur as we attempt to understand the history of the times through which we live.

John was conscious of our Lord's warning and projection of what lay ahead for the church: "There shall arise false Christs, and false prophets, and shall show great signs and wonders; insomuch that, if it were possible, they shall deceive the very elect" (Matt 24:24). That danger of deception was abroad in John's day, as it is in our own time. One aspect of it for John was the prevalence of a heresy that was known as Gnosticism, the details of which need not detain us, except to say the following. Gnosticism, in its various expressions, claimed that special knowledge existed, of a higher kind than was available to ordinary men or ordinary Christians, and which partook of a mystical element. (The Greek word underlying "Gnosticism" means "knowledge"). Its particular importance lay in its erroneous and heretical claims regarding the Person of Jesus Christ. At its base, it argued that there could not be a real union of the divine and the material, and that, therefore, there could not be such an event in the world as the union of the divine Son of God with human nature. Some argued that the man Jesus Christ was a human person to whom the Spirit of God had come in a special way, but that the Spirit departed from him before his death. Leaving aside more complex instances of the Gnostic system, such as a specimen known as Docetism, the upshot of it is clear. That was precisely what John was concerned about.

In short, what we are concerned with, in John's report as in our own time, is that the various expressions of "antichrist" are those that deny the real existence of the Son of God, incarnate in divine and human natures, in the form in which the scriptural revelation has presented him to us. It is the integrity of the biblical doctrine of the Person of Christ that is at issue. "Who is a liar but he that denieth that Jesus is the Christ? *He is antichrist*, that denieth the Father and the Son" (1 John 2:22).

The question we must ask, then, is "Who is Jesus Christ?" We have already looked at the answer in terms of the christological settlement that was reached by the church at the Council of Chalcedon in the year 451. The conclusion of Chalcedon was that in Christ, the Second Person of the eternal Godhead who came into this world to *become* Jesus Christ, the divine and human natures are joined in union "without confusion, without change, without division, and without separation." John, writing more than three centuries before Chalcedon, repeatedly set the true identity of Christ our redeemer at the center of, and as the determining orientation of, his thought and doctrine. The preface to John's gospel speaks for itself in that regard. And here in his epistle he drives home his point when he firmly erects the confession of the identity of Christ as the test of orthodoxy: "Every spirit that confesseth that Jesus Christ is come in the flesh is of God.

And every spirit that confesseth not that Jesus Christ is come in the flesh is not of God" (1 John 4:2–3).

The apostolic literature tells us that we are living in "the last time." In one aspect, the "last time" is to be understood as the church age that extends from Christ's first coming to his second coming. That is the age about which the entire book of Revelation is speaking and explaining to the church its preview of history. We are warned about the accelerating character of the age, when opposition to the gospel of God's grace is emerging in new and alarming forms and expressions. In our day, the heart of the antagonism against the gospel is a firm and deliberate rejection of what God has revealed regarding the Person of his Son, why he came into the world, and for what purpose he laid down his life on the cross. The various forms that heresy is taking in our own time warrant careful and detailed discussion beyond our present scope. But a particular result of the work of the antichrists as that affects the church is to be noted.

As anticipated in Matthew 24:24 which we cited above, false professors, false teachers and false ministries in the church have arisen. We should be aware of the ways in which such falsehoods can exist within the church and the damage they can do to the saints, even deceiving the elect of God if they are not alert and if, in the ultimate, they were not protected by the ministry in their lives of the Holy Spirit of Christ whom he has sent to them. The antichrists are the opponents of the gospel, and their nefarious intrusion into the church is capable of wreaking terrible damage to the continuity of the true witness of the church and to the lives of the saints. We are to understand that from the present time to the very end of this age the church and the purity of its gospel will be under attack by antichrists. For "We wrestle not against flesh and blood, but against principalities, against powers, against the rulers of the darkness of this world, against spiritual wickedness in high places" (Eph 6:12).

But what is it, then, that establishes the security of the true Christian who is in fellowship with God and which protects him against the falsehoods of the antichrists that are abroad? It is again the ministry to the soul of the Holy Spirit whom Christ sends to the Christian for that purpose. It is, in short, the "unction from the Holy One" (1 John 2:20). Christ is referred to as "the Holy One" in Mark 1:24 and by Peter at Acts 3:14. It is the unction that Christ sends to us by his Holy Spirit.

At this point particular care is necessary in understanding the meaning of what John is saying. First, this "unction [or this anointing, as in 1

The Christian's Highest Good

John 2: 27] of [or by] the Holy Spirit" is not to be understood as in some sense a special visitation of the Holy Spirit to certain individuals at certain stages of their progress in the Christian life and for certain special purposes. It is true and beyond doubt that the Holy Spirit does discharge his redemptive office in ways such as that. God does, at special times and for special purposes, pour out his Spirit on the church in a way that speaks to the largeness of his purpose for it. The times of revival in the history of the church speak clearly to the point.[2] But that is not what John is talking about in this context. For he is saying that this "unction" is something that every Christian has received. It is part of the endowment that makes the Christian a Christian. It is a part of the essential conveyance to the Christian of the grace of God that establishes him in fellowship with the Father, and without which the individual is not living "in the light" but is still "in the darkness." For John is here quite explicit in saying that it is precisely this "unction" of the Spirit that makes it possible to say that the person who is the beneficiary of it "knows all things." That does not mean, of course, that the Christian knows everything about every possible object of knowledge in this world. But he has a true knowledge of what his salvation and his reconciliation with God means and implies. The Christian, again, has "the mind of Christ" (1 Cor 2:16).

It is clear that the unction or anointing of the Holy Spirit that John is speaking of here is the property of all Christians by reason of the very fact that they are Christians, because there is no other way in which the Christian could have any true knowledge of the things of God. For as Paul the apostle has made clear, "The natural man receiveth not the things of the Spirit of God; for they are foolishness unto him; neither can he know them, because they are spiritually discerned" (1 Cor 2:14).

The argument we have just considered with the aid of John's epistle can be brought to a close by recalling John's insistence on the centrality of Christ. He makes his claim in that respect in a most interesting way. He says that "Whosoever denieth the Son hath not the Father." That expression is to be read in the light of the statement that we made at the beginning and which provides, as we are now observing at many points, the orientation of our thought on what we have called "the Christian's highest good." The highest blessing and privilege of the Christian, we have said, is that he

---

2. The following are minimal but significant elements of the large body of literature on this important point: Gillies, *Historical Collections*; Lloyd-Jones, *Revival*; Murray, *Pentecost—Today?*; Sprague, *Lectures*.

has been admitted to "fellowship with the Father and with his Son Jesus Christ." And we keep in mind that what we have said of that privilege applies to every Christian by reason of the fact that he is a Christian. He or she has "fellowship with the Father," and anyone who claims to have fellowship with God but is still "walking in darkness" is revealed as a liar. He is not speaking the truth. He is a sham. He lies and completely misrepresents himself (1 John 1:6).

The thrust of the argument at this point is that to deny that Jesus is the Christ is to deny the Father. That is so in the sense that to deny the identity of Christ as we have looked at it, in his eternal divinity and his substitutionary humanness, is to deny the entire deliberate purposefulness of God in his relation to sinful humanity. It not only denies the trinitarian identity of the Godhead, which in itself is revealed by the separate redemptive offices of the distinguishable Persons of the Godhead. It denies completely the sovereignty of God and his purpose of will in stating how sinful humanity can be again reconciled with him. But that, it is all too clear from the scriptural data, is the outgrowth of the naturally sinful state in which we are all bound as Adam's sinful progeny. The ultimate question confronting us is that of the locus of sovereignty. If a man asserts his imagined autonomous sovereignty, then he is saying in effect that God is dead. He has denied his own creaturehood, he then has no explanation of himself or anything else, and the darkness in which he lives will be found to be eternally impenetrable.

We who are the people of God must work out carefully, with all humility and in subjection to the word of God, the meaning of, and the ground of, the high privileges to which God has raised us. Everything that pertains to our relation with God, our reconciliation with him as we are raised by his grace from the pit of sin, and our destiny as we wait his call to the eternal glory, rests in the relevance of the Person and work of Christ. To answer the antichrists who would pull us down from the exalted status to which God has raised us we need firm and assured answers to two questions we have addressed at an earlier stage: Who is Jesus Christ; and Why did Jesus Christ come into this world?

seven

Mind, Heart, and Will

The Christian's highest good in this life, we have said, is discovered in the privilege that is accorded him of "fellowship with the Father." We began to look in the preceding chapter at some of the aspects of that fellowship as it is reflected in certain Christian distinctives. Those distinctives characterize the one who has that high privilege of "walking in the light" with the Father "as he is in the light" (1 John 1:3, 6). The fellowship inevitably has very practical implications. Fellowship with the Father is, on the part of the Christian, an intelligent fellowship that takes up all of the capacities and faculties of the individual soul. It engages the whole person, mind, heart, and will.

Those conclusions raise three questions: first, what are more precisely the intellectual implications of the Christian's fellowship with the Father; second, what moral and social implications also follow; and third, how can, and how does the Christian have, as the apostle John puts it, "confidence toward God" (1 John 3:21)?" Reflecting on the first question first, we shall find that the epistle of John again throws its light on our subject. We are not setting out in this way to offer a full exposition of John's epistle. That is a larger and more important undertaking than we have in view in these chapters. Our objective is more modest.

The Question of Mind or Intellect

Fellowship with God is an intelligent fellowship that is firmly based on the fact that the Christian knows certain things. In verses 12–14 of John's second chapter he emphasizes that those in fellowship with God are the beneficiaries of that privilege because "the word of God abideth in you" (1 John 2:14). John says further: "I have not written unto you because ye know not the truth, but because ye know it" (1 John 2:21). The engagement of the mind is to be seen as of primary importance in the progress of a person from the darkness of sin of which we have spoken to the life of light that God imparts. The point of doctrine warrants further consideration.

Our first parents, as they came from the hands of their Creator, were established in knowledge, holiness, and righteousness. For them, to *be*, was to *know*. Adam naturally knew God. In his act of self-awareness he was aware of God. In uncluttered friendship and openness of communion God walked with him the garden in the cool of the day (Gen 3:8). In holiness of mind Adam received and understood the special revelation of God to him. With his God-created faculty of emotion and affection Adam naturally loved God. With his will, still unbent and unbowed to the devil, Adam naturally obeyed God. In his pristine state, a harmony existed between the faculties of the soul, and by reason of God's constitution of Adam as a covenant creature, the mind, the intellectual faculty, was the prince of the faculties of the soul. Adam thought and spoke because God thought and spoke. Adam was the finite analogue of God, both as to his being and knowledge. But Adam fell. And the results of that fall were, in the first place, that the harmony of the faculties was shattered; and second, that the mind was no longer the prince of the faculties. Now the passions and the lusts ruled the soul, and Adam, in his false and disastrous assertion of autonomy, cast himself and all his natural posterity into bondage to Satan and sin. Adam denied his creaturehood, in that by repudiating his covenantal obligations to God he asserted that he was no longer subject to the criteria of life, knowledge, and behavior that God had communicated to him. Now, in his rupture of soul, he would find his criteria of truth and behavior excogitated from within himself and his own imaginations, or, as his life experience developed, in the social and cultural complex in which he lived. Such has been the sorry state ever since of all who have descended from him by ordinary generation.

Mind, Heart, and Will

The gospel of God's grace declares that those who turn to Christ in the saving faith and repentance that the Spirit of God imparts will be reconciled again to God. But what is to be said more particularly of the motion of the soul of a man to that new-born state? We have already stated the answer in expansive terms and have seen its terms spread liberally across the pages of Scripture. But it is to be said again that the first appeal of the gospel is to the mind. The mind that was hitherto "blinded by the god of this world" (2 Cor 4:4), but enlightened now by the Spirit of God, sees with previously unimagined clarity the truth of what God has said as to the man's natural state, the provision for rescue and reconciliation that God has made, and the need to fly to Christ for salvation. It is the enlightenment of the mind that is the first and crucial step in the process of renewal and conversion. By the regenerating grace of God the harmony of the faculties of the soul that was shattered by the fall is reestablished, and the mind again assumes hegemony, or the place of leadership, in the soul.

So it is that now in the Christian life, particularly as we are now reflecting upon the Christian's fellowship with the Father, it is with renewed mind that all of the blessings and privileges that are cognate with it are realized and appropriated by the Christian. That is why we say that the fellowship is first of all an intelligent fellowship. It is what it is because the Christian has been brought to *know* certain things. He has made a whole-souled response to the truth of what he now knows by God's enlightening grace.

It is worthy of brief digression to note that the section of John's epistle that we have just referred to (1 John 2:12–14) has been the subject of varying interpretation in the history of commentary. Many have concluded that here, as seems on the face of the text to be true, the writer is addressing three different classes of people: first, "little children," second, "fathers," and third, "young men." But other commentators have concluded that the designation "little children" is to be taken to refer to all of God's people in general. That would seem to follow from the fact that throughout his letter John addresses his correspondents as "little children."[1] If that is so, then these verses are to be understood as saying that after addressing God's people in general John then divides them into two classes for further counsel, namely fathers and young men.

But we don't need to stay with discussions on those levels. The important thing to be said is that here we have a further description of the people who, as John has had in view consistently, have been taken out of the

---

1. See 1 John 2:1, 2:28, 3:7, 3:18, 4:4, and 5:21.

The Christian's Highest Good

realm and kingdom of darkness and are now living in fellowship with God in the realm and kingdom of light. John is writing to them in these verses in order to say that he wants them to hold firmly to the high doctrines he has already addressed to them. He wants them to have a firm hold on their faith, to continue to know more deeply and influentially what they already know, because he has still more high doctrine to write to them about; and he wants to go on to show them the practical implications of what he is placing before them. What, then, is to be said about such people?

First, they are people whose "sins are forgiven for his name's sake" (verse 12). We have said that the first thing to be observed about the Christian is that he is a person who knows certain things. And here it is said that he knows that his sins are forgiven, he knows the manner in which, and the reasons why, his sins are forgiven, he knows the power of God within him to overcome sin as his walk with God proceeds, and he knows experientially that he enjoys the privilege of fellowship with God the Father.

Secondly, in the context of such knowledge the question arises as to the referent of the "his" in "his name's sake" in the text (verse 12). There is reason to conclude that it refers to God, and not directly, as might be thought, to the Lord Jesus Christ. That is because, again, the matter of fellowship with the Father is consistently in view here, as it is confirmed by the statements that "I write unto you, little children, because *ye have known the Father*" (verse 13), and "the word of *God* abideth in you" (verse14). But at the same time, of course, it is a vital part of the Christian's knowledge that it is for the sake of Christ and by the substitutionary redemptive work of Christ that our reconciliation with God the Father has been established. "The Son take(s) us by the hand and lead(s) us home to the Father."[2]

In such statements we have before us the common character, or characteristics of life, of all those who are Christian believers, little children (which, we have observed may refer to all believers in general), fathers, and young men. That is clear in the commonality envisaged in the statements: The fathers "have known him that is from the beginning"; the young men "have overcome the wicked one" and are thereby sure of their standing in Christ; and the little children have "known the Father."

We should note also the parenthetical nature of these verses. They stand between two important injunctions: first, a positive precept to "love the brethren" in verses 9–11, and then second, a negative precept in verse 15 and following, "Love not the world neither the things that are in the

---

2. Candlish, op. cit., 153.

world." Taking these verses as a whole, we may reflect on the reason why the apostle has inserted them in his letter at this point. It would seem that he wanted to emphasize and underline the fact that certain things were true of all of God's people, in the different classes he has referred to, that they must all hold firmly in common to the truths he had adumbrated and to the deeper doctrines he will go on to elaborate, in order that they will be armed and confirmed and enabled to live differently from the world around them. They are to bear witness to that world, but they are not to be identified with the world and its godless culture.

What the apostle says here applies to us all. We are all "little children." Our conversion makes us little children. "Except ye be converted, and become as little children, ye shall not enter into the kingdom of heaven" (Matt 18:3). That is, at our conversion we have been emptied of all pride in self, of all suggestions of self-righteousness. We have no merit or virtue in ourselves that could commend us to God, and in meekness and submission we have seen that our entire case, for now and for eternity, depends entirely on God's grace and love and eternal purpose in Christ his Son. As "young men," now grown strong in the faith and in the assurance of our salvation and adoption by God, we have learned how to follow after the things of God and to "grow in grace and in the knowledge of our Lord and Saviour Jesus Christ" (2 Pet 3:18). As "fathers" we have learned more deeply and more securely the profound truths of God's eternal covenantal purpose and his covenantal faithfulness. We have learned more of the relations between the Father and the Son who, in the redemptive council with the Holy Spirit, designed and established our redemption. We have seen and understood more deeply the meaning of the fact that "when the fullness of the time was come, God sent forth his Son, made of a woman, made under the law, to redeem them that were under the law, that we might receive the adoption of sons" (Gal 4:4–5). We know more fully the meaning of the Pauline summary that God has made us "accepted in the beloved" (Eph 1:6).

The true knowledge of the things of God that we enjoy is not in any sense due to our efforts of discovery. God does not exist at the end of a logical syllogism. As we know that *God is* because he has revealed himself to us, so all of the knowledge which as God's people we have come to possess is ours only because God by his gracious Spirit has revealed it to us. William Cowper has put it in familiar terms in his "God moves in a mysterious way": "Blind unbelief is sure to err / And scan His work in vain; / God is His own interpreter, / And He will make it plain."[3] We avoid, that

---

3. Cowper, "God moves in a mysterious way," in *Trinity Hymnal*, 128.

is, all temptations to rationalism that falsely imagines that the presupposed competence of unaided human reason is effective in searching out God. We banish all thoughts of incipient rationalism. We know what God has declared in his Word, we have believed the apostolic deposit of truth that is incorporated in it, and we have waited on the illumination of the Holy Spirit whom Christ sent in order to lead us into all truth.

Moral and Social Implications

Fellowship with the Father, to the extent that it is the property and right of those who "walk in the light" with him and is in no sense open to those who are still "walking in darkness," inevitably gives birth to further defining characteristics.[4] By what is now referred to as moral implications is meant the keeping of God's commandments; and by social implications is meant the relationship of love that exists between the people of God as they have fellowship with him.

John gives us a very important clarifying statement at this point. To understand what is involved at this stage we must keep in mind John's fundamental division of all people into two classes: those who now, by God's call and grace, "walk in the light" (1 John 1:7), and those who remain outside the realm of God's kingdom and still "walk in darkness" (1 John 1:6). That distinction is reinforced where John makes it clear that he is writing to people who know that "the darkness is past [or, more literally, is passing]" and that "the true light now shineth" (1 John 2:8). We have observed that fundamental dichotomy in Colossians 1:13, "delivered from the power of darkness, and translated into the kingdom of God's dear Son." The same basic conception and division underlie Peter's first epistle: "[God] has called us out of darkness into his marvellous light" (1 Pet 2:9).

When John says, "Hereby we know . . ." (1 John 2:3), that means that it is possible for the Christian to have a well-grounded assurance of his membership of the family of God, and John in this epistle casts his statements in such a way that they may be seen to be not only statements of character for those in fellowship with God, but at the same time tests of the genuineness of a claim to that effect.

---

4. As previously acknowledged, I am indebted for the thought underlying parts of what follows to the classic commentary by Candlish.

Mind, Heart, and Will

It is again useful to pause at this point to draw attention to what might seem a rather technical matter of the Greek language that influences our interpretation of the text. We note firstly that the pronouns "him" and "his" in 1 John 2:3 refer to God. "We know *him*," and "we keep *his* commandments." The same applies in the first half of the following verse, "I know him." The words are not to be taken to refer back to "Jesus Christ the righteous" at the end of the first verse of that chapter as might appear on the surface. The reference, when the context of John's total argument is in mind, is to the one whom the Christian now knows and with whom he is in fellowship. In other words, our interpretation is at this point anchored in the writer's conception of fellowship with God with which, at the third verse of the first chapter, he had began his epistle. The same applies to "*his* word" in verse 5 of John's second chapter and to "in *him*" at the end of that verse, "we know we are in him." It applies to God again in the "abideth in him" in verse 6.

But that raises the question of who is referred to as the "he" in "even as he walked" at the end of verse 6 of John's second chapter. "He that abideth in him [God] ought himself also to walk, even as he walked" (1 John 2:6). That final "he" clearly refers to Christ, whose walk provides, in John's immediate context, the example that the Christian in his own walk should follow. The change in reference in the personal pronouns to the "he" of Christ is confirmed by the fact that in the Greek text John uses a different word that is here translated "he." The word he uses can be translated literally as "that one," indicating a reference back to some person other than "God" as referred to in the immediately preceding text.

At several points in his epistle John is very firm in accusing as "liars" those who falsely claim to be members of the kingdom of God. He had used that strong language in the final verse of chapter 1, where he said that if we say we have no sin, then not only are we ourselves being untruthful but we make God a liar. We should then be making God a liar by disbelieving his promise in the preceding verse that if we confess our sin he is faithful and just to forgive us our sin and to cleanse us from all unrighteousness. At that point the "we" refers to Christians, to genuine members of the kingdom of God, who, for the moment, have fallen into sin. The context there was that of the Christian believer's progress in sanctification and the problem that sin, of various kinds and for various reasons, might enter his life. Now, in this fourth verse of his chapter 2, John is accusing as a "liar" the person who is making a false claim of fellowship with God. We make that interpretation because the context there is that of John's insistence on the character of those who do truly have fellowship with God. That is, they naturally and habitually keep his commandments. Against that, John says firmly that the person who falsely claims that distinctiveness is "a liar." John will return to the same very strong language of condemnation in the twentieth verse of the fourth chapter.

As a note of caution in interpretation, we note that we have in John's writing in this epistle what we have now seen as two levels of reference. There is, first, what is to be seen as his fundamental concern to distinguish throughout the difference in character of those who are properly entitled to fellowship with God and those who are not. But as we have seen, John writes out of a genuine pastoral concern for the true Christian believers, and he is conscious that in their walk with God in this world they may fall into occasions of sin. We should keep those two levels of reference in mind, at the same time as John's fundamental distinctions and differentiation of the true believer from the false is the principal determining motif of his work.

Now in expanding his context as we have just observed it, John argues that the person who is truly in fellowship with God will keep his commandments. That is his character. "In him the love of God is perfected" (1 John 2:5). The "love" here is not to be taken as primarily descriptive of God's love to us or our love to him, but as referring to the nature and quality of the relation involved in the fellowship with God, the Father and the Son. By that we mean that the entire ambiance or atmosphere in which that relationship exists is one of love, and the perfectness of it is referred to here in terms of the natural obedience to the law of God that the Christian exhibits in that relationship. The Christian walks in this world in the same manner as Christ walked, with a consistency, firmness, and determination. His whole soul is bent on obedience to God. He sees God in all things. He subordinates himself to God and the interests of the kingdom of God. He knows and thinks and lives in the way he does because he now has "the mind of Christ" (1 Cor 2:16). If a person who disregards and does not keep God's commandments nevertheless claims to know God he is, as has been said, a liar. He simply does not exhibit the character of those who have fellowship with God.

The relation of fellowship with God is reinforced by the apostle's reference to the "old" and the "new" commandments that now confront the Christian. To understand what is contained in the apostolic statements at this point it needs to be seen that there is no contradiction in the apostle's reference to the "old" and the "new." The "old commandment," as in verse 7 of John's chapter 2, is the "word" that John has previously addressed in the opening verses of his epistle. That commandment refers to all that John had said regarding those who walk in fellowship with God. The "new" commandment in verse 8 refers to the same thing. But it is said to be "new" because all that is involved in the relation of fellowship that John is speaking of repeatedly is seen and understood with an entirely new consciousness. That is, the "old" takes on a completely new perspective and significance, and it becomes "new" because we now see it in the context of our union with God in Christ. We now see in new perspectives the imperatives of obedience to the commandments. We are now "in him," to quote the writer's frequent explanation. Again in verse 8 John comes back to his fundamental explanatory conception, namely that the Christian no longer lives in the "darkness," but in "the true light." In all this, John is drawing a beautiful relation between doctrinal Christianity and experimental Christianity, between knowing the truth and living in accordance with the truth.

The distinction that underlies the privileges that we have seen to constitute the Christian's highest good, between those who are within the realm of the kingdom of God, or "in the light" and who walk according to its character, and those who are still in the realm of "darkness" and "walk in darkness," is naturally reflected in the character of the realm to which each belongs. The person who is within the kingdom will, with a new naturalness, love his brothers and sisters in the Lord. Of the person who is still outside the kingdom of God's grace, it is said that because he "hateth his brother, [he] is in the darkness even until now." The reality is that each individual will naturally exhibit and reflect in his life the character of the realm to which he belongs. The man who is still in darkness, who is in his unregenerate state and still outside of Christ, is simply and bluntly living a lie if he makes any pretense to knowing God.

A principal concern at this stage is that of the meaning of the mutual love that is being referred to. First, it is a ready recognition, by each person who is in fellowship with God, of the same character that exists in another. That is because each such person, knowing God and loving God, exhibits the love of God in himself or herself. There follows a mutual recognition and mutual affection. That mutual affection is the third of the characteristics of the person who lives in that highly privileged relation of fellowship with God. The first characteristic was doctrinal or intellectual, they know the truth. The second was moral, they keep the commandments of God. Before us now is the characteristic of love between the saints of God.

The Duty of Christian Love

We are asking what can be understood more precisely as the meaning of the "love" to which we have just referred. Whatever we discover it to mean, there is no doubt that it is to be understood in relation to, or in correspondence with, the love that God has for his people. In other words, we get at the meaning of love when we see that our love is to be like God's love, in the sense that it is an analogical reflection of his love or of the way in which he loves. We are to love because God loves, and in a way that reflects God's love. That essential reality is implicit in the apostle's argument: "Hereby we perceive the love of God, because he laid down his life for us" (1 John 3:16). That sixteenth verse is speaking of the love of God expressed in the atonement that his Son made on our behalf. It might seem on the face of it that such a sudden introduction of the atonement into this context of the way we should love each other is out of place and breaks up the sequence of the apostle's thought. But that is not so. We see very readily the reason for John's introduction of reference to the atonement when we see that the purpose of it is to establish the relation between the love with which God loves and what we are to grasp as the meaning of the love with which we are to love and emulate him.

Let us begin, then, with a statement about the love of God, or what is involved in his love. The first thing to be said is that God is the only One in whom love is self-referential. By that we mean that God loves preeminently in that he loves himself. On that very important point a comment from the puritan theologian, Stephen Charnock, is in order: "Holiness is the glory of the Deity . . . A love of holiness cannot be without a hatred of everything that is contrary to it. *As God necessarily loves himself* he must necessarily hate everything that is against himself; and as *he loves himself* for his own excellency and holiness, he must necessarily detest whatever is repugnant to his holiness."[5] In man, on the other hand, while he is the finite analogue of God, love cannot be, in the first place and preeminently, self-referential. The point to be grasped is that God, because he loves himself, loves his people because he sees in them the reflection of his own character and holiness. He loves in them what he sees of himself. But, it might be said, we have it on the authority of the word of God that he loved us while we were yet sinners,

---

5. Charnock, *Existence and Attributes of God*, 455, italics added.

and he sent his Son to die for us while we were sinners. Christ died, on the grounds of Romans 5:6–8, "for the ungodly." All that is quite true. But let us reflect on the fact that God has said to his people, "I have loved thee with an everlasting love; therefore with lovingkindness have I drawn thee" (Jer 31:3). We reflect, therefore, on the eternal love of God. And moreover, he set his love upon us in such a way that "he hath chosen us in him [Christ] before the foundation of the world" (Eph 1:4). Why God set his love on us as individuals, each in our particularity, is lost in the eternal dictates of his will. But he loved us from before the beginning because he saw us in Christ, and seeing us in Christ he saw us clothed with the robe of righteousness of Christ (Isa 61:10). He saw us as holy in him, brought by his Holy Spirit to the likeness of himself. God's love, moreover, in sending his Son as stated in verse 16, is a covenantally faithful, holy, total, and unchangeable love.

Now, John says, it is the obvious characteristics of those who have "fellowship with God" who, again, "walk in the light" and not "in the darkness," that they will love as God loves. That is, they will love each other because they see in each other the holiness of God and the sanctified beauty of the likeness to God in Christ, to which God had destined them and to which, with increasing intensity as time progresses, they are being brought. That is why we love, and what we love.

If that is what is to be understood as "love" in the sense in which it is to characterize the Christian and his status in fellowship with God, it follows that the "love" that we are speaking about is an attitude of affection that finds no place at all in the unregenerate person. Love, we are forced to conclude, must now be seen to involve a whole-souled motion of the person in which all of the faculties of the soul are engaged, intellect, emotion, and will. That, of course, is simply saying what is to be said of every Christian action. But the upshot of it in our present context is that only the regenerate people love. The nature and alignment of the faculties of soul of the unregenerate are such that considerations of self-interest, lust, and what the Scriptures refer to as inordinate affection, preclude love as the word of God has been seen to connote it.

But how, then, does or should that love come to practical and pragmatic expression? That, of course, moves the question to the necessary level of Christian ethics and conduct. And having now seen the meaning of love in its essence and its true being and identity, it is necessary to ask those very practical questions. How, then, does God's love for his people come

The Christian's Highest Good

to expression, and how, as the analogue of that love, must our love for each other be expressed?

First, the answer resides in the fact that God, having redeemed us to himself in Christ, directs his love to us in such a way that he is concerned about our well-being in all the affairs of our lives. He makes "all things work together for good to them that love God, to them who are the called according to his purpose" (Rom 8:28). And pointedly, it is true that because "He that spared not his own Son, but delivered him up for us all, how shall he not with him also freely give us all things?" (Rom 8:32). God having done the greater, in giving his Son for our redemption, will certainly do the lesser in conducting us to glory and providing for all our necessities as we are moved through this world and time by his Holy Spirit.

What, then, is the lesson to us? God loves us in that he has identified himself with our interests. He knows our concerns. He knows when we are in need and how his grace is to be directed to our needs. If we are to love each other with a love like his, then we, in turn, are to be prepared to identify ourselves selflessly with the interests of our brothers and sisters in the Lord. Shakespeare said it in an ordinary earthly way in one of his sonnets: "He that is thy friend indeed / he will help thee in thy need; / if thou sorrow he will weep; / if thou wake he cannot sleep. / Thus of every grief in heart / he with thee doth bear a part."[6] But we don't need the poets to guide us, true to the issue and meaningful though they may be. We have liberally spread through the pages of the word of God directives as to how we should live, and, in particular in the present context, how we should share one another's concerns and burdens.

One final point remains. God exercises his love toward us in such a way that he does not wait until we ask, or even, perhaps, until we are conscious that we need his help. He knows our needs and he prepares his answer to them before we ask. Is it not a mark of the likeness of our love to God's love that we don't necessarily wait for a brother's need to be announced and brought to our notice before we offer our aid? May we not take initiative and offer aid when we see it for ourselves? To what extent, in other words, are our necessities as Christian brothers and sisters mutually parts of our continuing concern?

The reference to Cain in the context of John's epistle (1 John 3:12) is, of course, an example of all that is contrary to love; so much so that the absence of love is capable, John says, of developing to the emotion of

---

6. Shakespeare, *Sonnets to Sundry Notes of Music*.

hatred and even murder. Cain was angered because his offering to God was rejected, whereas that of his brother was not.[7]

Such a development of hatred is characteristic of the world. The Christian will naturally be hated by the world. The world hated his Lord before him. That is clear from copious scriptural explanations. But the hatred is directed to the Christian precisely because of his likeness to God. We must understand that it is natural for the world, and for the men of the world, to hate the Christian. For the person who is still "in the darkness" and outside of Christ is in that class of people of whom Christ spoke when he said to certain of the Jews, "Ye are of your father the devil, and the lusts of your father ye will do" (John 8:44). Christ on that occasion referred to the devil as a "murderer from the beginning," and a progression toward the state of heart of the murderer is the natural outcome of hate as John is here speaking of it.

But when we have said that it is natural for the person of the world to hate, we say with equal firmness that it is natural for the Christian to love. That is the significant point of difference between the two. In the present context it would be a disastrous shame if the relation between the Christian and the world were misunderstood to the extent of diminishing the need for, and the characteristics of, Christian love. That necessity of love is to be expressed in the words: "As we have therefore opportunity, let us do good unto all men, especially unto them who are of the household of faith" (Gal 6:10). The obligation of "good unto all men" needs to be worked out carefully, and it opens up the possibility of misunderstanding the obligation of the church within the larger social and cultural complex of the common kingdom of which the Christian is a member, as distinct from the redemptive kingdom into which he has been brought by the grace of God.

The reference to "murderer" that we have noted is designed to alert the Christian believer to the danger of the extent to which a lack of love can go in dragging him down to a condition that is essentially like that of the world. A lack of love, or a careless attention to the demands of love, can lead

---

7. It is not directly apposite to our present objective, but it can be observed that Abel brought an offering, a blood sacrifice, that spoke to the realities of his *justification* before God. Cain, to the contrary, brought a grain offering, of the kind which, in the subsequent sacrificial system that God established in the Mosaic administration, was referable not to justification but to *sanctification*. The fallacy of placing sanctification or, that is, the imagined works of sanctification, before justification, and supposing thereby to gain favor with God, has been a continuing fallacy and danger in the church.

The Christian's Highest Good

to a condition not only of disregard for others' concerns and needs, such as our Christian profession should make us alert to, but it can spiral into an effective rejection of a brother and, in that, even to a disposition of heart and mind that is akin to that of the murderer. Such is the danger of carelessness in attention to the sound progress of our sanctification, or to our growth in likeness to the image of holiness that is in Christ. The demands of love emphasize that love must come from the innermost recesses of the Christian heart and character. We hear the words of James the apostle: "Be ye doers of the word and not hearers only" (Jas 1:22).

The Christian's ability to be faithful in this and in every other respect in which he is called to be like his Lord derives from certain basic characteristics of his position. The Christian is "in Christ," he has "passed from death to life," and he has eternal life abiding in him. But over and above all that, or essentially explaining the truth of those very facts, the Christian is a person in whom the power of God is at work. We saw that clearly before, when we referred to the "unction" or the "anointing" the Christian has received of the Spirit of God. We have it in Paul's letter to the Ephesians (Eph 3:20) that God is "able to do exceedingly abundantly" within us and for us, "*according to the power that worketh in us.*" And the same apostle recognized that what he was enabled to do in obedience to the calling of God was due to "his working, *which worketh in me mightily*" (Col 1:19). Therein lies the reasons for the Christian's success.

The characteristics of the Christian who is "walking is the light" emerge with what we may call a new naturalness because, in varying degrees and to varying extent, the character and holiness of God himself is reflected in the individual himself or herself. That is, of course, a high statement. But two things are to be said about it.

First, recall, as we referred to it at an earlier stage, that the Christian has been admitted to sonship of God. Recalling previous discussion, we are not established as sons because God has adopted us. We said that the opposite is true. God has adopted us because by reason of the new birth, being born again by the grace of regeneration, we are *sons of God by birth*. As born again by his Spirit we are partakers of his nature. By that new birth, born again by the Spirit of God, we naturally exhibit a likeness to the Father whose Sons we are.

Second, at this point we again observe a relation between doctrinal Christianity and experimental Christianity. By that is meant that while we hold to the *fact* of our sonship and the natural reflection of it, on the one

Mind, Heart, and Will

hand, the clarity and the persistence and the degree of recognizability of the *reflection of the fact* may and does vary. In other words, here at this important point we recognize that we each, who are beyond doubt God's people and who are safely within the realm of his kingdom of grace, may be less than diligent in cultivating the presence of God in our lives and possessing and reflecting the benefits of his grace. We can become careless in life and grieve him to whom we belong. And the intensity of our reflection of his goodness and glory may fade. But none of that destroys the fact for what it is. We who are God's people will, in one way or another and with a naturalness that cannot be mistaken, recognize and love each other for what we are.

But is it not possible that counterfeits might appear and for a time deceive even the elect? The answer is, of course they may. But our love for our brothers and sisters who, like us, are "in the light" and for whom in their own lives "the darkness is passing away" so that the light of God is progressively fashioning their lives (as it should fashion ours as we cultivate the presence of God) will come to expression in a mutual sympathy. That reality of sympathy cannot be overemphasized. We may recall that when we spoke of the heavenly high priestly office of Christ we observed that an element of that was our Lord's sympathy for his people still in this world and life. Similarly, then, the Christian's sympathy for his brothers and sisters is a reflection of the Christ likeness that should, and will in its varying degrees, reveal the development of his grace in our own lives.

But the case is different for the person who is still in darkness. The poor man walks in darkness, he doesn't know where he is going, the darkness has blinded him, and he is nothing but a cause of stumbling to his fellow men. What a terrible indictment! How thoroughly we should understand the meaning and the realities of sin that is abroad in the world and in the hearts of men. All is darkness to men who live in the dark.

The man who is aiming for heaven will not be a cause of stumbling. He will want to take others along on the journey with him. There will be lapses; lapses in our own walk with God and the pursuit of holiness. Our Lord said that "it must needs be that offences come" (Matt 18:7; Luke 17:1). Peter denied his Lord. One commentator has observed that "even the brother you love may be an offence, an occasion of stumbling, to you by the way." But we who live "in the light" are by God's grace to have "none occasion of stumbling within; to be purged of malice . . . to have the narrowing and blinding influence of the love of sin and the love of self exchanged for the

The Christian's Highest Good

broad, clear, free vision and action of the love of God, and Christ, and the brethren . . . to have 'the eye single' and 'the whole body' therefore 'full of light.'"[8]

8. Candlish, op, cit., 148.

eight

Abiding in Christ

On the night on which our Lord was betrayed, at his final supper with his disciples and in the context of his discourses to them, he spoke the parable in which he referred to himself as the "true vine" and his disciples as the branches. In that parable, our Lord referred to the two classes of people whose status and prospects we have addressed in the preceding chapters. We have referred to that dichotomy by contemplating those who are "dwelling in the light" and consequently have "fellowship with the Father," on the one hand, and those who remain in darkness and still "walk in darkness" on the other (1 John 1:5–7). In his parable Christ directs our thought in a similar way, first, to the true branches, those who have been truly united to him and will inevitably bear fruit to his praise; and second, to the false professors who, failing to bear fruit, will ultimately be destroyed.

The presence of false professors in the church is clearly acknowledged in the Scriptures. In the earlier Mosaic administration of the covenant of grace the nation was the church, and only a remnant of Israel, those to whom the Holy Spirit had conveyed the grace of regeneration, were members of the true "church in the wilderness" (Acts 7:38). As to the generality of the Israelites, the sins of idolatry and spiritual adultery were all too common among them. And so it has been ever since. "They are not all Israel, which are of Israel" (Rom 9:6). In our Lord's parable the branches that did not bear fruit were cast out and burned. Calvin comments at that point: "There are many hypocrites who, in outward appearance, flourish and are green for a time, but who afterwards, when they ought to yield fruit, show the very opposite of that which the Lord expects and demands from his people."[1] But the true branches will bear fruit, to the confirmation of their true status as joined to the vine and having the benefit of life-sustaining grace flowing from the root, which is Christ himself. The contrary case in our own time may occur in the false professors in the church who may have been admitted to membership on the grounds, perhaps, of an earlier baptism; but as the Puritan commentator Matthew Poole observes, "They are members of the visible church, and make a visible profession of adhering to him [Christ], with respect to their own opinion and persuasion of themselves, though they be not so in respect of any true, spiritual, and real implantation."[2]

The apostle John, speaking from the experience of a long life of pastoral ministry, observed the same phenomenon. Expanding on the seriousness of such situations by referring to what he saw as the "many antichrists" that were already in the world, he observed that "they went out from us . . . that they might be made manifest that they were not all of us" (1 John 2:19). And against that, John states the contrary fact, speaking to his "little children": "But ye have an unction from the Holy One . . . [and] the anointing which ye have received of him abideth in you" (1 John 2:20, 27). At that point in John's epistle he has very much in mind the important and necessary relation between the truth of God's revelation as it has been systematized in Christian doctrine and the working out of that doctrinal Christianity in practical and experimental Christianity.

The Christian's Abiding in Christ

In speaking now of the Christian's abiding in Christ, and of the necessary relation between that abiding and the continuing enjoyment of the blessing of God in the fruit-bearing conduct of the Christian life, we are not dealing with the nature of the high privilege of fellowship with God as it exists in and of itself. We have already referred to that at length. That means that we are not addressing any such question as to whether that fellowship is

---

1. Calvin, *Commentary on John*, 110.
2. Poole, *Commentary on Matthew–Revelation*, 358.

Abiding in Christ

terminable, or can be terminated, either from God's side or man's side, on the emergence of certain specifiable conditions or developments. Such a question is excluded by what we have already seen as the nature and character of the fellowship that God in his sovereign call to his people in Christ has established. Fellowship with the Father is established once-for-all for the child of God, and by reason of its nature it is indissoluble.

What we have at this stage, while it does not involve any prospect of the termination of the fellowship, is the obligation that rests on the Christian as he lives in this world within the context of that fellowship. In short, the Christian who understands the meaning of his high calling in Christ will strain every nerve to be faithful to the terms of the relationship with God that is thereby established. The fellowship with God exists interminably by reason of the very nature of Christianity. But it carries with it obligations of faithfulness on the Christian's part. The Christians are being told that if they continue to hold fast to what they have heard and believed, or if, that is, they remain true to the experiential implications of their confession, then they will "continue in the Son, and in the Father" (1 John 2:24).

But we have said that the relation of fellowship with the Father and the Son will, in fact, continue because, it having been established on the grounds we have inspected, it is indissoluble. It might appear, then, that we have here an internal contradiction. The fellowship with God and the blessings it conveys is said to be indissoluble, and yet we are told that the enjoyment of those blessings is dependent on the Christian's continued abiding in Christ.

But there is, in fact, no contradiction. While the Christian believer's union with Christ and the fellowship with the divine triune God that is implicit in it are firmly established, it is necessary for the Christian to see with equal clarity the responsibilities for life that the relationship with God involves and carries with it. In essence we have here the same injunction as Peter states when he says: "As he which hath called you is holy, so be ye holy in all manner of conversation [or conduct of life]; for it is written, Be ye holy; for I am holy" (1 Pet 1:15–16).

But another aspect is prominent. While the fellowship of which John speaks repeatedly cannot be broken or annulled, the Christian can, by his conduct and careless disregard, lose the joy of the relationship. John had written earlier that his wish was that the Christian's "joy may be full" (1 John 1:4). He knew that the true and truly born again Christian can all too easily lose the joy of the position which, by divine purpose, actually belongs to him. The Psalmist David, in his great penitential psalm spoke not about the loss of his salvation, but the loss, as he put it, of "the joy of thy salvation" (Ps 51:12). So it is with the Christian.

But how can that be so? Let us put it in the form of another question. The apostle says in the following verse that God has promised us eternal life (1 John 2:25). But do we always and consistently meditate upon and truly grasp the meaning of that "eternal life"? And in doing so, do we let that meaning sink into our consciousness in such a way that it determines our existential response and action? John goes on to say that he is speaking to the Christians in the way he is because he is concerned with "them that seduce you" (1 John 2:26). So then, the issue becomes that of whether we as Christian people are alert to the seductions to sin that are abounding around us in the world. That is the pressing issue. The question is whether we have a sufficiently acutely developed sensitivity to the occasions of sin that can tarnish our relation of fellowship with God.

What is sin? we should ask ourselves. And what are the occasions or elements of sin that most readily drag us down from the height of the joy and complacence of fellowship with God? We can each answer those questions for ourselves. We can each know the meaning for our own lives of Paul's statement to the Colossians, "As ye have therefore received Christ Jesus the Lord, so walk ye in him" (Col 2:6). We know well the same apostle's plea to the Romans, "Be not conformed to this world; but be ye transformed by the renewing of your mind, that ye may prove what is that good, and acceptable, and perfect will of God" (Rom 12:2). Paul is there anticipating the argument of John in this epistle: "Love not the world, neither the things that are in the world" (1 John 2:15).

But there are two further and highly significant points of relevance. First, the pleasure of our fellowship with the Father is very much two-sided or reciprocal. God the Father, as does the Son, takes pleasure in the fact that the relation of fellowship exists between him and us. As Christ looks on us and sees us as the "travail of his soul, and is satisfied" (Isa 53:11), so the Father, who ever looks on his "beloved Son" and is "well pleased" (Matt 3:17), looks on us whom Christ has redeemed and he, too, takes pleasure in us. Should it not be clear that if we by our sin tarnish the fellowship with the Father, then he, God in his triune identity, is grieved? For we have it clearly in Paul's letter to the Ephesians: "Grieve not the holy Spirit of God, whereby ye are sealed unto the day of redemption" (Eph 4:30). And does not the fact that we as God's people are "sealed unto the day of redemption" speak

Abiding in Christ

again to the truth that we have already explored, namely that our very relation of reconciliation with God and the fellowship with him to which we have been introduced is also interminable, unalterable, and secure for all eternity? How, then, should we live?

Second, in this whole matter of sin in the life of the believer and the tarnish it places on our fellowship with God, we have what we may call the paradox of the Christian's progress in sanctification. On the one hand the joy of fellowship with the Father grows increasingly real in the Christian's consciousness as that progress continues. But at the same time there grows within the believer's consciousness also an increasing sensitivity to sin, a growing realization of unworthiness before God, a deepening understanding of the meaning and the subtleties of sin, and a higher awareness of the need for repentance before the throne of God. It is the advanced saint who knows most clearly that he is a sinner, and that his standing before God, his fellowship with God, is due only to the unmerited favor of God set forth in Christ his Son.

In the twenty-seventh verse of his second chapter, in a sentence that begins with the word "But," John makes an important adversative statement. It is set against the preceding statement of obligation and encouragement to live according to the implications of the fellowship with God that the Christian enjoys. John has pleaded with the Christians to whom he wrote to be true to those obligations and responsibilities, and now he expresses his confidence that they will, in fact, be faithful. A twofold statement of confidence is made at that point. First, John calls on the Christians to "abide in him [God]," and second, he states the reason why they will be faithful, namely that the "anointing which ye have received of him abideth in you" (1 John 2:27). The text harks back to what we noted earlier as the "unction from the holy One," which is here explained more fully as the "anointing" of the Spirit whom Christ sends to his people. That unction or anointing abides with the Christian, the truth and the knowledge of it that the Spirit imparts therefore abides with him, and by reason of that the Christians "abide in him [God]" (1 John 2:27). The unction, or the anointing, that is contemplated here is the fulfillment of the promise that our Lord had made: "If I depart, I will send him [the Comforter] unto you. . . . When he, the Spirit of truth is come, he will guide you into all truth. . . . He shall glorify me; for he shall receive of mine, and shall show it unto you" (John 16:7, 13–14).

The Christian's Highest Good

In other words, we see in these verses a most interesting projection of John's thought. He has established so far the two things we have looked at: first, the permanence and irreversibility of the relation of fellowship between God and the Christian; and second, the assurance, by reason of the Holy Spirit's endowment of unction, of the Christian's faithfulness to that fellowship. Here, then, John projects his thought to the future condition that will inevitably follow. In doing so he anticipates and builds an expository bridge to what he will say in the following chapter. That future, which is now assured to the Christian, contains, as John states it here, two realities. First, the Son of God will return; and second, the Christian, because he has been faithful, will "not be ashamed before him at his coming" (1 John 2:28).

The logical and very necessary experiential result follows. In anticipation of what becomes the climax of the thought, namely the realization of the coming again of the Son of God to whom the Christian is even now joined in indissoluble union, John states that "Every man that hath this hope in him purifieth himself" (1 John 3:3). John closes his argument with the simple but profound and far-reaching statement that lies at the heart of the Christian experiential mandate. He must be like his Lord. As Christ is "righteous" and just and pure, so must his servants be also.

The active righteousness of Christ has been placed to the repentant sinner's account and he has now been established in a state of justification in the accounting of God. But now there is something more that is characteristic of the true Christian. It is something that gets down behind the meaning and the possibility of the state of justification to which he has been introduced. It is that the Christian has been "born of him" (1 John 2: 29). A wonderful and inexpressible work of the Holy Spirit's ministry to the soul has taken place. The Christian has been "born" into the kingdom of God. We saw in an earlier context that that birth established the Christians as the sons of God. We put that by saying that we are not sons of God because God has adopted us; but we are adopted into the family of God because he has made us *sons by birth*, having been born again by the Spirit of God himself. Now, it becomes imperative, the Christian must work out in his life the implications of the state of righteousness that God has granted to him for Christ's sake. The Christian, that is, must pursue with diligence his progressive sanctification.

But the call to the Christian to "abide in Christ" is rendered problematic, we have seen, by the occasion of sin. In our discussion in chapter 4 of the Christian's highest good we referred to the subtlety and the hideous nature of sin, and to the Christian's need to be aware of the danger of being

Abiding in Christ

trapped by it. Recalling our previous comments only briefly, why, we may ask, does the Christian sin? The answer lies in the nature of the identity and the practical life of the Christian.

Consider again the Christian's regenerate status. Regeneration is that secret, sovereign, and unsolicited work of the Holy Spirit, whereby the faculties of the soul, the mind, affections, and will, are endowed with abilities and capacities they did not previously possess, and a new disposition or principle of action is implanted in the soul. The Christian is a new person, created anew by the fact that he is born again by the Holy Spirit of God. Because he is "in Christ, he is a new creature; old things have passed away; behold, all things have become new" (2 Cor 5:17). "Our old man is crucified with him [Christ]" (Rom 6:6). But the faculties of soul have not yet been made perfect. They are capable of attack by the forces of evil, and the Christian may for a time and on occasions entertain old habits, old thought-forms, and old allegiances, and he may be dragged down by them to a level of life that is lower than that of the privilege to which he has been raised in Christ.

The Christian sins when he allows himself to neglect for a time his attention to the means of grace—prayerful communion with God, meditation (more than a cursory reading) on the word of God; the prayerful participation in the administration of the sacraments, notably the Lord's Supper; and the fellowship of the saints. Less than careful attention to the means of grace may elicit the lament that the hymn writer, William Cowper, put as follows: "Lord, it is my chief complaint / that my love is weak and faint; / Yet I love Thee and adore; / O for grace to love Thee more"[3]

But as to the Christian's temporary entrapment in sin, the very tenor of his life is as John describes it: "Whosoever abideth in him [Christ] sinneth not. . . . Whosoever is born of God doth not commit sin; for his seed remaineth in him; and he cannot sin, because he is born of God" (1 John 3:6, 9). Two negative statements are in order. First, the statement does not point to the possibility of perfection in righteousness in the Christian in this life. A doctrine of so-called Christian perfectionism has troubled the church at times in the past, but need not detain us at this time. Second, we cannot moderate the seriousness of the statements being made in the text by saying that what is intended is simply that the Christian will refrain from known or deliberate sin. More is intended in the claim that the one that is born of God does not commit sin.

---

3. William Cowper, "Hark, my soul, it is the Lord," in *Congregational Praise*, 374.

How can that be so? The explanation of what is involved is that the true child of God *cannot consent to continue in sin*. That reality is reciprocal with the reality that the Christian's union with Christ is indissoluble and unbreakable. Moreover, the underpinning of the Christian's refusal to continue in sin is that the "seed" of God is in him. God's deposit of faith, that follows as the gift of God inherent in his Spirit's work of regeneration in the soul, has led to the impartation to the renewed sinner of aspects of the very nature of God; not, of course, God's essential nature or, that is, his eternal essence, but the likeness to him that the conveyance of his communicable attributes connotes. Moreover, what is said at that point reflects again what was said in verse 27 of chapter 2 of John's epistle; namely, that the underlying reason for the Christian's perseverance and faithfulness is that "the anointing which ye have received of him abideth in you." It follows that there should be no misunderstanding or deception in the Christian's mind. Righteousness of character will be reflected in righteousness in action and life. And righteousness in action reflects the identity of those who are joined to Christ.

Confidence Toward God

We have distinguished at several points between the fact of the Christian's high status of fellowship with God, on the one hand, and the actual experiential awareness in the life of the Christian of the joy which that fellowship implies and carries with it. In his life in the world as he walks with Christ, the Christian believes and rejoices "with joy unspeakable and full of glory" (1 Pet 1:8). That is true in a wonderful and fundamental sense. But in the grind of everyday, there are interruptions to the joy. God has ordained tests and trials for his people. He disciplines them, and with kindness keeps on with his ordained plan to conform them to the image of holiness that he has set forth in his Son. In the heat of the day, the Christian cannot always and readily see the reasons for the plan. He is finite. He realizes often only with hindsight the active love of God who "makes all things work together for good to them that love God, to them who are the called according to his purpose" (Rom 8:28).

We addressed previously what we termed the moral and the social implications of fellowship with God the Father and his Son Jesus Christ. Those who have been brought by his grace into that high state of fellowship with him, who are now "walking in the light" and no longer "in the darkness," will keep his commandments (the moral test) and will love one another (the social test). That, as is well known from a familiar reading of John's epistle, has frequently been the emphasis of commentary on it. The apostle states that God with whom we have fellowship grants our requests "because we keep his commandments" (1 John 3:22); and God is propitious to us because "we love one another, as he gave us commandment" (1 John 3:23). That is because "he abideth in us by the Spirit which he hath given us," intimating again that our knowledge, our obedience, and all our joy in God in Christ are grounded in the "unction" or the "anointing" that we have received from him. All that is very true. But the question often persists in the Christian's mind as to whether he is, in fact, truly a participant in the right of enjoyment of all such benefits. Existential questions that can assume large proportions, even in the truly born-again Christian mind, call for response. The aspect that particularly engages us is that of the grounds of the Christian's assurance of his title to all that has been described as his highest good.

Throughout his letter John had spoken many times of that important question of the Christian's assurance. For example, at the beginning, immediately after he had laid down his high doctrine, he says "Hereby we do know" (1 John 2:3). And later, "We know that we have passed from death to life" (1 John 3:14). Again, "Hereby we know" (1 John 3:19). But lest all such argument should still leave the Christian in any doubt about his status, and lest that should be understood only on the level of mere intellectual apprehension, John speaks to the issue by addressing the believer at the very heart of his being. "If our heart condemns us," he proceeds to argue in the twentieth verse of his third chapter, and "If our heart condemn us not" in the following verse. Something is being said here about the conscience, the judicial faculty that either disturbs or calms the heart, the very innermost recesses of the Christian's being and the very seat of the determinants of his action and life. How can he be sure that with "confidence toward God" (1 John 3:21) he can rest in the love of God that is of the essence of Christian fulfillment? What, in short, are the grounds of Christian assurance and confidence?

First, we know that we have eternal life because we have believed the doctrines. On the very lowest level, that doctrinal test is of primary importance. We know, with an honest self-awareness that came through the shock of self-realization, when the Spirit of God convinced us of our lost estate of sin and misery, that our only hope of life was in Christ Jesus and his substitutionary atoning work. We believed the doctrines of God's revelation at that point, and we recall the joy of release from the burden of guilt and sin that we knew when we knelt before the cross of Christ and thanked him for the greatness of his redemptive work for us.

At that climactic point in our lives we knew that what God has said in his word was true. We saw that we did, in fact, sustain real and immense obligations to him and his law. We saw that that law was righteous and good. We understood that we had sinned against God, that we stood in a wretched state of sin by reason of the very fact that we were who we were, and that if there was no way of reconciliation with him we stared only into a gaping eternal perdition. Perhaps we had read the gracious statements of his word many times and had heard them preached as often. But they had then no penetrating meaning for us. Now, with a new level of understanding that inflamed our consciousness only because the light of God had shone into our hearts (2 Cor 4:6), we knew that what God had said to us all along was, in fact, the true explanation of both the death of sin and the source of life in Christ. Our hearts burned with a reaching out to God that was hitherto incomprehensible to us. We fled to Christ. Our conscience told us that the life we now found in Christ was the very door to eternal bliss and security in the presence of God. The first ground of assurance is grounded in the fact that we know and believe the doctrines.

Second, the Christian's assurance properly follows from his self-evaluation of his new relation to the law of God. He is well aware of the fundamental necessity that the prospect of eternal life turns on obedience to law. The Christian knows, again with a conviction that has burned itself into his very heart and soul, that he is wretchedly unable to keep the law of God with that total integrity that fulfills all of the law's demands. But he knows also, and he knows with a conviction that has grown to become unshakeable, that he is completely absolved from guilt because Christ has paid all of the penalty of all of his guilt and sin. What a glorious substitution, his heart has told him. So that now, still conscious of his inability to keep God's law perfectly, he knows that he loves the law, and with a new confidence he prays for the guidance and support of God's Spirit that he might yet be more consciously obedient to the law. So that, to the first test of life, the doctrinal ground of assurance, the Christian adds the assurance grounded in his new relation to the law.

Third, assurance of eternal life is grounded for the Christian in the realization he has that though again his practice may fall below his intentions he has a love for his fellow believers. That necessity of love between the saints of God comes to expression in many ways. Whose company, for example, is the Christian most pleased to enjoy? The fellow saints or the people of the world? Where does his comfort lie? Where does he feel a kinship and rapport? Where, to put it in the most ordinary terms, does he become aware of rest of heart and soul, or if you like, of psychological comfort? So that, the assurance grounded in love of the brethren is added to that of intellectual or doctrinal belief and that of the love of the law of God.

Fourth, the Christian, because he now exists and lives in new regenerate personhood, knows in his times of self-evaluation that he is aware of levels of truth and understanding that were previously completely foreign and in no respect understandable to him. The truth of which he is now conscious is vastly wider than that of his own salvation. It expands to the divine revelation of God's extensive covenantal purposes. He sees with a new conviction of conscience that he has been translated by no less a power than that of the Spirit of God himself into a new estate for him, and for the church of God to which he has now been introduced, that was ordained to the glory of God before the foundation of the world. Why is that so? he asks himself. Why is he now, in his very being and levels of consciousness, what he was not before? Why is the very range of his conceptions different from what he has ever been able to describe? The answer to all such questions rests in the fact that the Christian, the ordinary Christian (if any Christian can be said to be ordinary; the very expression is wide of the mark) – every Christian, and not only some who, perhaps, have advanced to a particularly high state of fellowship with God, has been blessed by God with the "unction" or the "anointing" of the Holy Spirit. So that, added to the doctrinal, the legal, and the social test of love, the ground of the Christian's assurance of eternal life rests in the testimony of the Spirit of God to him.

Fifth, our puritan fathers spoke frequently of what they referred to as the "practical syllogism" as a ground of Christian assurance. We summarize that as follows. Consider, first, the major premise: Only those who are the true children of God will or can perform the works that God requires and that please him; or, that is, perform the works of progressive sanctification. Second, now add the minor premise: The Christian, in honest and humble self-awareness and self-evaluation before God, recognizes in himself the marks of such works. Then third, from the logical conjunction of those major and minor premises the conclusion follows that therefore the individual concerned is a true child of God. So that, to the doctrinal ground, the legal ground, the ground of love, and the witness of the Holy Spirit, the Christian legitimately adds the ground provided by the practical syllogism.

We can bring together those last two grounds of Christian assurance by observing the statement of the apostle Paul to the Romans: "The Spirit itself beareth witness with our spirit, that we are the children of God" (Rom 8:16). It is important to note that the text does not say that the Spirit of God bears witness *to* our spirit. It says *with* our spirit (the compound verb in the Greek text at that point makes it unarguably clear that the preposition "with" is the necessary translation). The doctrine at issue, then, is that there is a parallel form of witnesses to our Christian status. First, there is the witness of our own personal consciousness such as we have already discussed; and second, parallel with that and accompanying and confirming it, is the witness of the Holy Spirit.

Two further things follow from what has just been said. First, the phrase "if our heart condemn us" at 1 John 3:20 points to the danger of self-deception. There were some people at that earlier time, as John explained in verse 19 of his second chapter, who were eventually exposed as false professors. Their heart in due time condemned them, they were then condemned by the church, and they left the church. It is possible for one to be deceived, and that because, as we have seen, the devil and the adversary of the soul may present himself as an angel of light. How, then, can one be sure that "his heart does not condemn" him? Two reasons are relevant. First, it is the "heart" that is being spoken of in this context; not simply a superficial intellectual cognition, but the full recesses and faculties of the soul that give their response after full and serious examination. And second, as a result and outcome of that full examination of the soul, the conscience, or the judicial faculty, is operative and engaged. The conscience is the moral monitor of the soul. A large part of the moral problem of the non-Christian is that his conscience has become dulled. Their conscience, as Paul stated it to Timothy, has been "seared with a hot iron" (1 Tim 4:2). Paul could say of himself, on the other hand, that he had "a conscience void of offense" (Acts 24:16). Now the Christian, as result of the self-examination we have spoken about in the preceding comments on the Christian's assurance, can know with a calm honesty before God that his conscience does not condemn him.

But secondly, it is important to be sure in the presence of God that our heart does not condemn us! Is there any residual sin that has remained unconfessed? Has our love for the brethren been tarnished by any slight or foolish antagonism? Has our love for the law of God in any sense slackened, such as to diminish our wish for its reflection in our lives? Has any sense of self-aggrandizement diminished in our consciousness the priority of the sovereignty and the glory of God in our lives? If, on any such levels and on more that might be contemplated, our heart in any sense condemns us, we cannot enjoy and express the "confidence" in our coming to God that we are here speaking about.

What, then, is the outcome of our argument? We have seen from many aspects the high privilege of fellowship with God. The Christian has not only been granted new life in Christ. He has not only been granted the new identity as a son of God. He has not only been privileged to come into the very throne room of God. He not only has available to him all of the benefits and privileges that accrue to the sons of God. The Christian can experience even something higher. It is, as the apostle John states it at the twenty-first verse of his third chapter, that the Christian can have and enjoy all of that with "confidence."

That means that there is no barrier between God and his new-born sons that need diminish the freedom and "joy unspeakable" (1 Pet 2:8) of the fellowship. We are not speaking here, of course, of any such erroneous imagination that might suggest that we are in some mystical way absorbed into the very essence of God. Far from it. The very realization of who it is with whom we have to do as the eternal and all holy God banishes the thought. But we are speaking here of a new freedom of approach to God, an intimacy of communion with him in his presence. We begin to see what the writer of the letter to the Hebrews had clearly in view when he said that we may "come boldly unto the throne of grace" (Heb 4:16). And we begin to understand what the apostle Paul was speaking about when he said that "in Jesus Christ our Lord . . . we have boldness and access with confidence" to God (Eph 3:11–12). As God's people we realize, that "God is greater than our heart," he knows all about us, he has marked out our journey for us, he "knows all things," and he wants us to come to him with all of our cares and concerns, but with a "confidence" such as that with which a trusting child comes to his Father. What boundless grace, what unspeakable blessing God the Father has conferred upon us his people.

But we are to build upon what has already been said, that we may "assure our hearts *before him [God]*," and that with "confidence" we may come into the presence of God. Here we have what we are to understand as the nature and quality of the prayer life of the Christian. But what is prayer? It is not a mere repetition of certain phrases, or expressing certain desires, or expressing beautiful thoughts. It is first of all humiliation in the presence of God, a total adoration of God above all else, a recognition of the glory and majesty and ineffable holiness of God who dwells in the light that no man except his loved ones can approach. It is a thankfulness for all of the grace and benefits that God in his Son and by his Holy Spirit has given us, a recognition that all of our days and all of our ways are in his gracious hands; and only then does prayer contain petitions for our needs. So that the essence of prayer is the realization simply that we are in the presence of God, that we are "before him."

With that realization clearly in view we know that "whatsoever we ask we receive of him" (1 John 3:22). What is the scope and intent of what is in view in that statement? The answer is to be found by looking, first, not at the possible subjects of requests or the objects of desire, but at the relationship between the Father and the Christian who is invited to bring his requests to God. If the praying Christian knows that in his prayer he is in the presence of the eternal God, and if in that act and position he is conscious of all that has been said about his relation with God, surely his words will be careful and in all respects in submission to the will of God. How could a mere man, raised to the status of sonship with the eternal God though he is, ask or desire anything in the presence of God other than what is consistent with the will of God? The true Christian, who has learned how to come into the presence of God and how to conduct himself with all reverence in that presence, will want for himself nothing other than what God in his eternal and wise ordination has already prepared for those that love him. Whatsoever, then, is asked of God will be received, because what is asked will be according to the will of God. Indeed, the very requests that are then made known to God the Father will have been created in the individual soul by the Holy Spirit himself. That is what is meant by petition and intercession in prayer.

When prayer is understood in such terms as those we can see why John in this context speaks of the "heart," and whether or not the "heart" condemns us. For when we stand or kneel in the presence of God it is the innermost self, the very heart of our being, that is exposed before him. It is with the heart that God has to do; we are at that point naked before him; we are then completely in his hands, without reserve on our part, with God in control; and with open face and with humble submission we wait his answer to our prayer in the conviction he conveys to us by his Spirit that we are asking within his will, and that he has taken pleasure in us and our conference with him.

That final statement to be made in this connection, which has to do with God's conveying to us the conviction and assurance of his Holy Spirit, is confirmed by the apostle: "Hereby we know that he abideth in us, *by the Spirit which he hath given us*" (1 John 3:24). We are introduced here to the great doctrines of the Person and work of the Holy Spirit, into which it is not possible to enter at length at this time. But two things can be said briefly in conclusion. First, by reason of the redemptive office of the Holy Spirit, which he undertook in the council of the Godhead before the foundation of the world, every Christian believer has received the Holy Spirit within himself: "For by one Spirit are we all baptized into one body" (1 Cor 12:13). Second, in the discharge of his redemptive office the Holy Spirit conveys to those for whom Christ died the gifts and benefits of his atonement that he purchased for them. Those benefits, as we have now seen, include a freedom and confidence in access to God the Father. "For through him [Christ] we have access by one Spirit unto the Father" (Eph 2:18). What a remarkable extent it is to which the grace of God has "more abounded" (Rom 5:20) to us as Christian people who are now joined to him in Christ.

nine

The Christian's Prospect

The preceding chapters have considered principally what we have referred to as "the Christian's highest good." That highest good is that the Christian in this world is accorded the privilege of "fellowship with the Father and with his Son Jesus Christ." That highest good involves, in its ultimate respect, the fact that the Christian will see God. That blessing, which will become the joy of the eternal age, awaits the coming again of Christ when all those whom he redeemed will hear the words: "Come, ye blessed of my Father, inherit the kingdom prepared for you from the foundation of the world" (Matt 25:34). Then we shall see God in the face of his Son in his glorified human nature. Though with the eyes of flesh in this life we cannot *see* God, our highest good is to *know* God and to have fellowship with him. We know him as he has revealed himself in his word, in various other ways and most notably in his Son, as his essence is displayed in the disclosure of his attributes, and as we come to him in communion, adoration and worship, prayer, and petition.

In this final chapter our thought turns to the eternal prospect that lies ahead for the Christian. Paul the apostle was eloquent in his conception of the eternal joys that await the saints of God. "For me to live is Christ," he said, "and to die is gain" (Phil 1:21). Paul, whose thought was consistently christocentric in the highest degree, glorified Christ and the cause of the kingdom of Christ in his life. Now his death would be gain in that he would see his Lord face to face. For him, his death would mean that he would be

The Christian's Highest Good

"*with* Christ; which is far better" (Phil 1:23). William Hendriksen has observed that "gain for Paul can never be dissociated from gain for the cause of Christ, for the one objective in which Paul rejoices most is that in *his* person Christ may be magnified. Death will be a distinct gain because it will be the gateway to clearer knowledge, more wholehearted service, more exuberant joy, more rapturous adoration, all of these brought to a focus in Christ."[1] The clear-sighted view of Paul had taught him to say that "whilst we are at home in the body, we are absent from the Lord" (2 Cor 5:6), and in his present state, and apart from his desire to serve his Lord in the avenues of his appointment, he would rather be "absent from the body, and present with the Lord" (2 Cor 5:8).

The apostle John entertained the same conception: "Beloved, now are we the sons of God, and it doth not yet appear what we shall be; but we know that, when he shall appear, we shall be like him; for we shall see him as he is" (1 John 3:2). But now, in this present life and pilgrimage and with the common apostolic confession, "We walk by faith, not by sight" (2 Cor 5:7). Given that confession, what, we should ask, is meant by the statement that we "walk by faith," or more precisely, what is the meaning of "faith"?

Faith, in briefest terms, is assent based on adequate evidence. Faith is not a non-rational action, an activity that bypasses the contribution of any faculty of the soul. It is an action taken by the *person* whose responsibility it is, and because *full personhood* is engaged in it, it necessarily issues from the engagement of all of the faculties of the soul. That means that there is an intellectual content in the expression of faith; there is an emotional content; and the exercise of faith is an act of responsible volition. That is consistent with what we have observed previously as the meaning of the regeneration that the Holy Spirit of God effects. By that sovereign and unsolicited action, we have seen, the faculties of the soul are endowed with abilities and capacities they did not previously possess, a new and holy disposition is planted in the soul, and as a result an individual is brought to faith in Christ. The voluntary exercise of the capacity to believe, in the faith which has been conveyed to the individual, is a whole-souled action; the assent on adequate evidence that it involves follows the consent of the mind that now, in the regenerate person, has been reestablished as the prince of the faculties of the soul; an intellectual consent is made to what God has said in his revealed word; it involves the expression of new affection for God as he has revealed himself in Christ; and the movement to Christ in faith is made

---

1. Hendriksen, *Philippians*, 76.

freely with a new and recreated volition. "Thy people shall be willing," the Psalmist has said, "in the day of thy power" (Ps 110:3).

When it is said that now we walk by faith, the faith to which we refer is a believing activity of the whole person. It takes up the concurrent and jointly-determined action of all of the faculties of soul. But that action is what it is because the Holy Spirit has recreated in the soul a harmony between the faculties. We observed previously that the result of Adam's fall, in one of its most serious aspects, was that the previous harmony of the faculties was shattered, at the same time as the hegemony or leadership of the intellectual faculty of mind was displaced; the passions and lusts now ruled the soul. What is being said now is that an outcome of the Holy Spirit's act of regeneration is that the harmony of the faculties has been restored, and in the Christian person the mind is again supreme. While that is so, the Christian in his walk with Christ will become progressively aware of those realities. That, in short, is an important aspect of the Christian's realization of his progress in sanctification.

As to the faith by which the Christian walks, Matthew Poole has judiciously commented that "it is a real, present, confident assent of the soul of a believer to the promise of God by which the spiritual good things to come, and which fall not under sense, yet with a most vehement and intense desire urged for, are made to have a mental, intellectual existence and subsistence in the soul which exerciseth it."[2]

When He Shall Appear

"When he shall appear," John says, "we shall be like him" (1 John 3:2). The prospect of that eschatological reality burns its intensity in the believer's soul. It might be noted that some expositors have observed that as the words, "when he shall appear," follow immediately after "it doth not yet appear what we shall be," a different translation might be preferable at that point. The pronoun "he" in "when he shall appear" might be more properly translated, it is said, as "it" or "that." We would then have "When it shall appear," or "when that shall appear." The alternative translation of "it" is suggested in the margin of the English Standard Version of the Scriptures. In that case, what is referred to in the "shall appear" phrase is not understood to be Christ, as most translations assume, but what was previously

---

2. Poole, *Commentary on Matthew-Revelation*, 860.

held in mind in the phrase "it does not yet appear." What is being said, on that translation, is that when that which has not yet appeared is finally disclosed and does appear, then we shall be like him, meaning by the "him" God himself. The case for such an alternative translation and exegesis of the apostle's statement at this point regarding the final prospect of the Christian is strongly argued by the nineteenth-century Scottish exegete, Robert Candlish.[3]

In any event, the apostle John has alerted us to the glorious consummation of the Christian believer's redemption and the prospect of his inheritance in the new heaven and the new earth (Rev 21:1). The aged apostle had climbed the heights of fellowship with his Lord. He had been with him on the mount when Moses and Elijah had appeared. He had leaned on his breast on the night on which our Lord was betrayed. And now he reminds his readers of the companionship they share with him in the beatitude to which his Lord had called him. He acknowledges that they with him have been raised to that high plateau that the apostle described to the Ephesians as "accepted in the beloved" (Eph 1:6). Beloved in Christ; accepted into closest confidence with the Father; what heights of elevated bliss the grace of God has conveyed to those whom he has redeemed, and that at no less a cost than the dying in our nature of his beloved eternal Son.

Well might John exclaim: "What manner of love the Father hath bestowed upon us." We note that John refers here explicitly to the love of the *Father*. He casts our minds back, as he himself must surely have contemplated it, to the predeterminate council of the Godhead before the foundation of the world, in which the triune Persons in their distinguishable identities, Father, Son, and Holy Spirit, undertook to assume distinctive redemptive offices for the salvation of their elect. It is true that when we pray "Our father which art in heaven . . ." we are addressing God in his triune Personhood. It is the triune God who is Father of his adopted sons and who wishes that his will might be done on earth as it is in heaven. But John has spoken throughout his epistle of the respect in which we are privileged to have fellowship with the Father, explaining that that carries with it fellowship with the Son and the Holy Spirit. And now in this present context the momentum of his thought is focused on the Father to whom, as Paul put it, "we, through Christ, have access by the Spirit" (Eph 2:18). That orientation of thought is confirmed by John's more expansive conclusion later in his epistle, when he says that the love of the Father "was manifested

---

3. Candlish, op. cit., 281–83.

The Christian's Prospect

toward us" because he "sent his only begotten Son into the world that we might live through him" (1 John 4:9). At that point, in order to underline the vastness of the love of the Father to us, John speaks of the Father's love that he is now bringing clearly before us in his third chapter. Again, "In this was manifested the love of God . . . that he sent his Son to be the propitiation for our sins" (1 John 4:10).

Why, we may ask, has the Father loved us? It is certainly not because we had, or could have had, any merit that should call forth such love and complacence of the Father toward us. He loved us and chose us out of the good pleasure of his will. There is no more ultimate explanation of anything in sentient or inanimate reality than the will of God. We cannot enter into its ineffable determinations. We bow before him and worship. But John is here expanding the meaning of the Father's love, the indescribable vastness of it, by reminding us that he has called us to be "the sons [literally 'children'] of God (1 John 3:1). We have spoken already in different contexts of the fact that we who belong to God have been raised to the status of sons. We are sons of God *by birth*, we have seen, by the new birth by the Spirit of God that raised us to new life. We do not rehearse those earlier discussions at this point. But we take note of the implication of the fact that John brings before us at this point.

There is a distinctiveness about the sons [children] of God, John is saying, a profound difference between those who, to hark back to John's introduction to his epistle, are walking with God in the realm and "kingdom of light" and those who are still "in the darkness." Such is the remarkable unity of conception in this brief epistle. The distinction comes to expression in the fact that "the world knoweth us not, because it knew him not" (1 John 3:1). The ignorance and blindness of the natural man in sin is all-too-clearly revealed and confirmed and spread liberally across the pages of Scripture. (See 2 Cor 4:4; 1 Cor 2:14). It reached its height when the Jews to whom Christ came, his own people who "received him not" (John 1:11), completely failed to recognize that they "crucified the Lord of glory" (1 Cor 2:8).

But the direct reference in the phrase "knew him not" is to be taken to refer to the absence of knowledge of God. The world does not know Christ and God the Father by Christ, John is saying, because they have, and can have, no conception or understanding of who he, God, is. It is true, as the first chapter of the letter to the Romans makes clear, that every man knows that God is, and that they have some conviction of the power and

The Christian's Highest Good

majesty of God. But that "knowledge" rests on the level of mere cognition, and every time it rises unbidden to the level of consciousness it is pushed down, suppressed, and smothered by human imaginations and predilections (Rom 1:18). But John is saying here that the natural man who is still "in the world" has no understanding at all of Christian personhood. We should realize that the entire system of thought-forms, worldviews, and epistemological and moral criteria of truth reside, for the non-Christian, on an entirely different level from that of the Christian.

We observe further in relation to the first verse of this third chapter of John's epistle that, as is implicit in what has been said, God has "*bestowed his love upon us.*" That is, God the Father has not only loved us in some abstract sense, without bringing the practical and experiential implications of it to bear on our lives. In an ultimate sense, that bearing of practicality is brought to expression in the very fact that because of the propitiation that his Son offered for us (1 John 4:10, 2:2) God is now at peace with us (Rom 5:1). But the "bestowal" of his love means that his love is active, it directs our days by the Spirit whom he sends to be our guide and comforter, and it marks out the ways of all of our days for us. God, having saved us and reconciled us to himself by his Son, does not then leave us to ourselves. His continuing love is such that by his Spirit-filled works of providence he orders all things for our good, including in that remarkable "all things" our final destiny in the eternal kingdom of glory that we shall share with him in his Son.

We have discussed in earlier contexts the sonship that elevates the apostle's thought in these verses. We recapitulate briefly three aspects of what is involved. First, the Christian enters into the status of sonship by reason of his new birth by the Holy Spirit. Second, as the text states, it has not yet been disclosed to us fully all that we shall be and enjoy when our redemption is complete and we share the eternal kingdom with God in Christ. It is true that the obvious statement that "Eye hath not seen, nor ear heard, neither have entered into the heart of man, the things that God hath prepared for them that love him" (1 Cor 2:9) has primary reference to the benefits of the Christian life in this world. But there is in it, of course, a reference also to what it is that remains to be revealed to the Christian when he enters the realm of eternal glory. And that, John is saying, has not been revealed and cannot be revealed.

But third, one thing can and must be held clearly and dearly by the Christian. That is that when Christ appears "we shall be like him; for we

The Christian's Prospect

shall see him as he is" (1 John 3:2). It bears repetition that the text is not saying that our seeing Christ in that great day will make us like him. For all will see him, many seeing him not as Lord and redeemer, but as judge, and they will dread his presence; they will see his glory displayed, but they will not see him "as he is," in the respect that he is full of grace and the friend of sinners. The truth is that we shall see Christ as he is because in this life and our walk with God the Holy Spirit has been at work in our lives making us gradually and progressively like Christ in holiness and conformity to the will of God. The judicious comment by Matthew Poole also bears repetition in this connection: We are "therefore by that likeness *qualified* for such vision" as we will have of Christ when he comes.[4]

What, then, should be the Christian's response to the high status as a son of God that he has become in Christ, and to the manifold blessings and benefits that accrue to him as a result in this life? John introduces his discussion of that question by the summary but imperative statement: "Every man that hath this hope in him [Christ] purifieth himself, even as he [Christ] is pure." At issue here is the large question of the Christian's progress in sanctification as he "works out [the meaning of] his salvation with fear and trembling" (Phil 2:12).[5] The imperative at this stage is that the Christian, because he realizes the fact of his union with Christ for what it is, and because he holds the confident expectation of his fuller likeness to Christ at the day of Christ's return, should not only see and act on the relevance of that to his life in this world, but he should live with an unwavering desire to do so. That should be the mark of his life.

The imperative of the Christian life is that we are to be followers, in the sense of imitators, of Christ. In saying that, we are not falling into the modern unorthodox trap of imagining that the sole purpose of Christ's coming into the world was to provide for us an example of the way in which we should live. That heresy has often given rise to the assumption that all that is necessary to establish peace and rectitude in the world is for everyone to apply the ethic of the Sermon on the Mount. That suggestion is, of course, quite wide of the mark. That ethic cannot begin to be understood, let alone applied, by the non-Christian person. What we are saying here is, first, that it was the pure and sinless Son of God who lived and died for us as our redeemer; and second, because he has redeemed us to himself we are to

---

4. Poole, op. cit., 934.

5. Refer to the more detailed discussion in chapter 5, "Christ Our Sanctification," in Vickers, *Being and Belief*.

The Christian's Highest Good

be like him in the purity of character that was his. That objective in our own lives, we know only too clearly, will be realized to the full degree, and then imperishably for all eternity, only when Christ returns and we see our Savior face to face.

In the meantime, the Christian is to realize that the moral law of God, which has been crystallized in the Ten Commandments, remains his rule of life. Is it possible that we shall keep that law perfectly? The answer is clear from our own consciences. Sin, we have plenty of occasion to know, is too strong for us except we live with and by the sustaining grace of God and the ministry of his Holy Spirit. But by that gracious ministry he provides for us a way of escape from every temptation (1 Cor 10:13). That being given, there does not follow from it any reason why, because we are saved by grace, we should "continue in sin, that grace may more abound" (Rom 6:1). But it is to be said of the Christian person that he loves the law, and that by the grace given freely to him he strains every nerve to live according to the law. It is an established fact of the Christian life that when the Christian sins he knows he has sinned. And indeed, the conviction of sin, followed by the disgust that the Christian feels for sin, is in itself a mark and a sign that he is a true child of God.

The argument that we should be like Christ follows from the truth that John has repeated frequently and which we have taken as the orientation point and principal concern in our studies. The fellowship with the Father accrues from the fact that by the regenerating grace of God by his Holy Spirit we are joined to Christ, in a vital, spiritual, and indissoluble union. We are, as John states it at the very end of his epistle, "in him [God]" because we are "in his Son Jesus Christ" (1 John 5:19–20).

That union with Christ and sonship of God mean, as Peter states it, that we are "partakers of the divine nature" (2 Pet 1:4). That does not mean, of course, that we begin to share in God's *essential* nature, in the sense that we become divine and share in God's essence, or that regeneration involves our divinization. But it means that, as in the case of human nature where the character, and even, often, the idiosyncrasies, of the father are reflected in the son, so in the more elevated case we are now speaking about, the character of God our Father will be reflected in us, his sons by our new birth. It is inevitable that there should be a common nature between God and us. One scholar, commenting on the similar verse in James 1:18, "Of his own will begat he us," observes that "we are born of God, by an inward communication of his nature to us."[6]

---

6. Candlish, op. cit, 270.

The Witness of God

When God saves the sinner, makes him his son by birth and a "joint-heir with Christ" (Rom 8:17) and joins him in union with himself in Christ, he gives that person gracious and vivifying signs of his new-born status and confirmations of his promises to him. We looked in a previous chapter at several ways in which the Christian may reflect on the grounds of his assurance of his standing in Christ. Those grounds culminated in the testimony to the individual of the direct witness of the Holy Spirit. The witness of God is explored further in the conclusion of John's epistle, and it will be useful to look at the manner in which he makes his final appeal to his readers.

As John draws his epistle to a close he elevates the Lord Jesus Christ as the source of life and as the one by whom God has communicated his purposes and intentions. From the very first verse of his epistle John had made it clear that all that he would go on to say would be what he had received from "the Word of life." The Second Person of the Godhead is the Word of God who was in the beginning with God and was God (John 1:2). God has always spoken to us only in his Son. He came into the world to "declare" the Father to us (John 1:18). And now John sums up the matter by stating that "God has given to us eternal life, and this life is in his Son. He that hath the Son hath life" (1 John 5:11–12). Because Christ lives in us by his Spirit, we share the life that is in him. "As the Father hath life in himself, so hath he given to the Son to have life in himself" (John 5:26).

We may observe further the manner in which Jesus Christ as the Son of God is elevated in John's concluding chapter. First, "This is he that came by water and blood, Jesus Christ" (1 John 5:6); second, "the witness of God, which he hath testified of his Son" (verse 9); third, "He that believeth on the Son of God hath the witness in himself" (verse 10); fourth, "the Son of God is come, and hath given us an understanding" (verse 20); fifth, "we are in his Son Jesus Christ" (verse 20). As a background to all that John says in these verses, he presents a fundamental argument in the second last verse of the chapter: "The Son of God is come, and hath given us an understanding" (1 John 5:20). It is that "understanding," the work of the Spirit of God on the mind, the intellectual faculty of the soul, that is vitally important in the witness of God to the Christian person.

John's objective in these verses is to emphasize God's *witness* to us his people. His central statement is contained in verse 9 where he refers to "the witness of God," and the "witness" that John has in view is stated as that "which he hath testified *of his Son*." We note that in verse 6 John writes: "It is the *Spirit* that beareth witness, because the Spirit is truth." John is recapitulating the relationship between the Son and the Holy Spirit. For the Spirit is the Spirit of the Son, in that he is sent by the Son from the Father. That, as John had understood it in his gospel, is the fulfillment of our Lord's promise to his disciples. "I will send him [the Holy Spirit] unto you" (John 14:7), and "when he, the Spirit of truth, is come . . . he shall glorify me; for he shall receive of mine, and shall show it unto you" (John 14:13–14).

Given the centrality of the Person and work of Christ in John's conceptions at this stage, he refers to Christ as "he that came by water and blood" (verse 6). The "water" refers to the occasion of Christ's baptism, and the "blood" refers to his sacrificial death for us. We see here two things. First, in these verses the triune nature of God is revealed. It is *God* whose witness is placed before us, meaning in John's terminology in this epistle God the Father; it is the Son, the second Person of the eternal Godhead, about whom the witness is made; and it is the Holy Spirit, the third Person of the Godhead, who is the conveyor of the witness. We know that at the baptism of Christ the Father and the Spirit were present; first in the Father's statement of his pleasure in the Son, and then in the Holy Spirit's appearance in the form of a dove.

It is worthy of note that while we have referred the "water" in the text to the occasion of Christ's baptism, several alternative meanings have been assigned to it in theological discussion. Some have referred the "water" to the purity of our Lord, and his "blood" is then referred to his death which acquired its salvific efficacy by virtue of the purity or sinlessness of the redeemer. Some have referred the "water and the blood" to the water and blood that flowed from our Lord's body when it had been pierced as he died on the cross, understanding that as referable to John 19:34, "One of the soldiers pierced his side, and forthwith came there out blood and water." Others, for example John Owen, understand the "blood and water" to have reference to "justification and sanctification."[7] But it would seem that the exposition as we have given provides the most harmonious explanation, given that the apostle is directly concerned in these verses with the testimony that is borne to us by the Person and life and work of our Lord Jesus Christ.

We note that there has been some dispute in the history of commentary, based on variations in the Greek manuscripts, regarding the correct

---

7. John Owen, *Communion with God*, 10.

translation of verses 7 and 8. The English Standard Version appears to reproduce the generally accepted judgment of the textual critics that verse 7 should read simply: "there are three that testify [or, as KJV has it, that bear record]," and then verse 8 should state the three testifiers, namely "the Spirit, the water, and the blood." It is said in the text that "these three agree." That is, they each bear witness to precisely what John's context here is saying as to the witness of God. They together confirm that it is the Person and work of Jesus Christ that provides the ground on which God the Father can and does communicate to his people the benefits and blessings of the redemption that Christ accomplished for them.

The second thing to be seen in this context is that John's reference to the "blood" of Christ contains implicitly all that the apostle has already said regarding the efficacy of the atonement that Christ offered, and it is by reason of that sacrifice of the Son that "God hath given to us eternal life, and this life is in his Son" (1 John 5:11). The reference to the "blood," moreover, confirms again John's previous argument that the sign of true belief is the recognition that "Jesus Christ is *come in the flesh*" (1 John 4:2). The "in the flesh" stands against the false philosophies of the Gnostics of John's day, as it points to all that Christ did in his sojourn in the flesh for our salvation. John has held before us in this epistle the full humanity as well as the eternal deity of our Lord. John had exhibited that in the opening verses of the epistle.

There are two further statements in John's epistle at this point that warrant careful attention. First, the significant implication follows in verse 10 of chapter 5 that "He that believeth on the Son of God *hath the witness in himself.*" That conclusion harks back to what John had stated at length in verses 20 and 27 of his second chapter. He referred there to the "unction" or the "anointing" of the Spirit." When we considered that issue of the witness of the Spirit, we saw that it constituted one of the several grounds on which the Christian's assurance should be seen to rest. God does not leave his new-born child to himself. He ministers to him by his Holy Spirit. He works out the way before him. By his Spirit, God ministers all grace to him and accomplishes within him that holiness without which, as the letter to the Hebrews states it, "no man shall see the Lord" (Heb 12:14). By that ministry of his Spirit he conducts his children safely to glory.

In that connection we may observe that the statement in verse 9 that the "witness of God" is "greater than the witness of men" points to the highly significant fact that the witness or testimony borne by men is necessarily, in the nature of the case, external, based on their own observations and interpretations. But the witness of God is not external, but internal. That, moreover, is precisely the character of the Spirit's witness to us. The Spirit works his illuminating work within the very recesses of the soul, operating on and in all of the faculties of soul that had otherwise continued in the darkness that Satan had imposed on them. The internal testimony of the Spirit bears witness to the one, Jesus Christ, who, as this entire epistle of John proclaims, is in the believer. We are "in God" as we are "in Christ" and he is in us. John had said the same thing at verses twenty-one and twenty-three of the seventeenth chapter of his gospel.

Second, John here brings his argument back to a point he had made throughout his epistle regarding those who are still "walking in darkness." In verse 10 of his final chapter he contemplates again the possibility that a person who is "walking in darkness" may falsely claim that, like the true children of God, he has "fellowship with the Father." But John's indictment in such a case is severe. It is not simply that such a person is himself a "liar," but the much more terrible fact is that he has "made him [God] a liar." Here again John is reflecting the very conceptual structure of his epistle as that was stated at the beginning. The fact that in such possible instances the action of man should throw in the face of God that he, God, is untruthful amounts to the blackest blasphemy. We who are God's people have not only been rescued from such a terrible possibility, but because we have "believed the record God gave of his Son" (verse 10), we are now secure in him.

Conclusion

A small number of issues are worthy of final statement. We observed at the beginning of our studies, and we have carried the statement throughout at many points, that associated with the reality of the Christian's highest good is the fact that there are only two classes of people in the world. It is clear from the very central doctrines of our faith that there are regenerate and there are unregenerate people. The form in which that has come to issue in our studies is that, taking a theme from the first epistle of John, there are those who are "walking in the light" and are in "fellowship with the Father and his Son Jesus Christ," and there are others who are still "in darkness" and are "walking in darkness." Two final things are to be said in that connection.

The Christian's Prospect

First, the "fellowship with the Father" to which we have referred as the Christians' highest good, is indissoluble, interminable, and unbreakable for those who have been admitted to the privileges of it. In particular, it has been emphasized that the occasions of sin in the lives of those who, by reason of their new birth have been admitted to those privileges, do not destroy the fact that such people are still "walking in the light." But it does mean that the joy and the comforting realization of fellowship are tarnished. And the terrible reality is that in their sin they are sinning as people who are in fellowship with the Father. It is in their new nature that sin is committed. That is a measure of the shame of sin. Sin in the Christian life grieves the Holy Spirit; it is an affront to the God who has assumed us into that high relationship with himself. The consequent realization is calculated to lead, on the sinning saint's part, to contrition and the repentance that follows.

Second, if we have understood with any depth the reasoning that has occupied John in his epistle we can readily understand his statement regarding his purpose in writing. It was, he said, "that ye may know that ye have eternal life" (1 John 5:13). "Believing on the name of the Son of God," John says in the same verse (though that particular clause is thought by many textual critics not to have been part of the best Greek text), is precedent to eternal life. Life is in the Son. And we acquire eternal life by belief and trust in him. John has made the point extensively, both in this epistle and in his gospel.

It is useful to reflect on the entire body of doctrine and the plea for the practical application of it that John has presented, and, in doing that, to bring together the Godward and the manward aspects of the cause and process of salvation. The *efficient* cause of salvation, as John reminds us in his references at various points to the sovereignty of God, is the grace of God. The *meritorious* cause is the Person and work of Christ. And the *instrumental* cause is the exercise of faith. That faith, as John has encouraged us to understand it, is a belief and trust in the merits of Christ's substitutionary life and death. Saving faith, which is always the whole-souled response of the sinner to the invitation of Christ to come to him, is necessarily made up of assent to the truth that God has declared, based on the knowledge that the Spirit of God imparts, and a whole-hearted trust of oneself to Christ and reliance upon his veracity in his stated invitation and his appointment by the Father as the Savior of sinners.

The Christian's Highest Good

John reminds us of the high privilege we have by reason of our adoption as sons [children] of God, in that "whatsoever we ask, we know that we have the petitions that we desired of him" (1 John 5:15), and that by the supervising ministry of his Spirit he will not allow us to continue in sin (1 John 5:18).

But let us ask ourselves, can we grasp the extent, the wonder, and the vastness of the love of God to us? John gives us some assistance when he forces us here to realize that "the whole world lieth in wickedness" (1 John 5:19). If the scope, the destructive darkness, and the terrible emptiness of all the godless claims of the world could engage our awareness for what they are, how we should praise and glorify God in our worship of him that he has rescued us and joined us to himself in a remarkable embrace of spiritual life. If something of the meaning of "the world" could burn itself into our consciousness, we would realize the extensiveness of the referent in the final verse of John's epistle: "Little children, keep yourselves from idols" (1 John 5:21). How can we who belong to God do less when we have been brought to know that Christ died our eternal death in order that we could share with him his eternal life?

Finally, it is impossible to bring our discussions to a close without adducing again, as we have already done on several occasions, John's conclusion that we not only "*know* him [God] that is true," but the greatest thing of all is that "we are *in him* [God] that is true." The ground on which that can be said, and on which it is to be said with complete confidence by the Christian believer, is the fact that such a person is "in his Son Jesus Christ."

That magnificent conclusion to the epistle, as we saw at the beginning of our studies, is to be set against the corresponding statement in the third verse of the first chapter. At that initial point John said that the thing that would orient and give form to his epistle was the fact that the highest blessing of the Christian life is that we have "fellowship with the Father and with his Son Jesus Christ." Now that he has reached his conclusion he reprises his opening motif and explains it all by saying that we are "in God" and "in his Son Jesus Christ."

John, in his epistle, maintains the perspective he established at the beginning and understands that there are just two classes of people: those who, by virtue of God's regenerating grace, are "walking in the light," and those who still "walk in darkness." The words of our Lord himself, in his declaration of self-identification, reinforce the claim. "I am come," he says, "a light into the world, that whosoever believeth on me should not abide

The Christian's Prospect

in darkness" (John 12:46). And "I am the light of the world; he that followeth me shall not walk in darkness, but shall have the light of life" (John 12:8). The Christian heart rings with the apostolic strain: "Thanks be unto God for his unspeakable gift" (2 Cor 9:15). We are now "in Christ," in vital, spiritual, and indissoluble union with him.

May God grant that by his grace we might yet learn how to walk more closely with him as he marks out his way for us in this short, uncertain life and earthly pilgrimage.

Bibliography

Abrams, M. H. *The Norton Anthology of English Literature*. New York: Norton, 1962.
Alexander, Cecil Francis. "There is a Green Hill Far Away." In *Trinity Hymnal*, 256.
Bavinck, Herman. *Reformed Dogmatics: Volume 2: God and Creation*. Grand Rapids: Baker Academic, 2004.
Beeke, Joel R. "The Apostle John and the Puritans on the Father's Adopting, Transforming Love." In Joel R. Beeke, *The Beauty and Glory of the Father*, 79–105. Grand Rapids: Reformation Heritage Books, 2013.
———. *The Beauty and Glory of Christ*. Grand Rapids: Reformation Heritage Books, 2011.
Berkhof, L. *Systematic Theology*. Grand Rapids: Eerdmans, 1939.
Bidwell, Kevin J. "Losing the Dance: is the 'divine dance' a good explanation of the Trinity?" In Iain D. Campbell and William M. Schweitzer. *Engaging with Keller: Thinking Through the Theology of an Influential Evangelical*, 97–133. Darlington, UK: Evangelical Press, 2013.
Blamires, Harry. *Recovering the Christian Mind: Meeting the Challenge of Secularism*. Downers Grove, IL: InterVarsity Press, 1988.
Bultmann, Rudolph. *Jesus Christ and Mythology*. Norwich, UK: SCM Press, 2012.
Calvin, John. *Commentary on the Epistles to the Corinthians, Volume Second*. Translated by John Pringle. Grand Rapids: Baker, 1979.
———. *Commentary on the Gospel According to John, Volume Second*. Translated by William Pringle. Grand Rapids: Baker, 1979.
Campbell, Iain D. and William M. Schweitzer. *Engaging with Keller: Thinking Through the Theology of an Influential Evangelical*. Darlington, UK: Evangelical Press, 2013.
Candlish, Robert S. *A Commentary on 1 John*. Edinburgh: Banner of Truth, 1973.
Carson, D. A. *Becoming Conversant with the Emerging Church: Understanding a Movement and its Implications*. Grand Rapids: Zondervan, 2005.
Caswell, Edward. "Jesus the very thought of thee." In *Trinity Hymnal*, 645.
Charnock, Stephen. *The Existence and Attributes of God*. Minneapolis: Klock and Klock, reprint, 1977.
Congregational Praise. London: Independent Press for the Congregational Union of England and Wales, 1951.
Cowper, William. "God moves in a mysterious way." In *Trinity Hymnal*, 128.
———. "Hark, my soul, it is the Lord." In *Congregational Praise*, 374.
Cunningham, William. *Historical Theology*. 2 vols. Edinburgh: Banner of Truth, 1960.
Descartes, Rene. *Discourse on Method and The Meditations*. Various editions.

Bibliography

Dunson, Ben C. "Do Bible Words have Bible Meaning? Distinguishing Between Imputation as Word and Doctrtine." *The Westminster Theological Journal* 75, 2 (2013) 239–60.

Estelle, Bryan D., J. V. Fesko, and David VanDrunen. *The Law is not of Faith: Essays on Works and Grace in the Mosaic Covenant*. Phillipsburg, NJ: P&R Publishing, 2009.

Eveson, Philip H. *The Great Exchange: Justification by faith alone–in the light of recent thought*. Leominster, UK: Day One Publications, 1996.

Fishler, M. "Protagoras." In Dagobert D. Runes, *Dictionary of Philosophy*, 257. Ames: Littlefield, Adams, 1958.

Frame, John M. *No Other God: A Response to Open Theism*. Phillipsburg, NJ: P & R Publishing, 2001.

———. *Systematic Theology: An Introduction to Christian Belief*. Phillipsburg, NJ: P&R Publishing, 2013.

Geehan, E. R. *Jerusalem and Athens: Critical Discussions on the Theology and Apologetics of Cornelius Van Til*. Philadelphia: Presbyterian and Reformed, 1971.

Gillies, John. *Historical Collections of Accounts of Revival*. Edinburgh: Banner of Truth, 1981.

Greene, Theodore, M. "The Historical Context and Religious Significance of Kant's Religion." In Immanuel Kant, *Religion Within the Limits of Reason Alone*, ix–lxxviii. Translated by Theodore M. Greene and Hoyt H. Hudson. New York: Harper, 1960.

Hendriksen, William. *New Testament Commentary: Exposition of the Gospel According to John, Volume 2*. Grand Rapids: Baker, 1954.

———. *New Testament Commentary: Philippians*. Edinburgh: Banner of Truth, 1962.

Henry, Matthew. *An Exposition of the Old and New Testament: New Testament Vol. I*. London: James Nisbet, 1857.

Hodge, Charles. *A Commentary on 1 & 2 Corinthians*. Edinburgh: Banner of Truth, 1974.

———. *Systematic Theology*. 2 vols. New York: Charles Scribner, 1873.

Horton, Michael. *The Christian Faith: A Systematic Theology for Pilgrims On the Way*. Grand Rapids: Zondervan, 2011.

Hughes, Philip Edgcumbe. *A Commentary on the Epistle to the Hebrews*. Grand Rapids: Eerdmans, 1977.

———. *Paul's Second Epistle to the Corinthians*. Grand Rapids: Eerdmans, 1962.

Kant, Immanuel. *Critique of Practical Reason*. Translated by Thomas Kingsmill Abbott. New York: Barnes & Noble, 2004.

———. *Critique of Pure Reason*. Translated by J. M. D. Meiklejohn. New York: Barnes & Noble, 2004.

———. *Religion Within the Limits of Reason Alone*. Translated by Theodore M. Greene and Hoyt H. Hudson. New York: Harper 1960.

Keller, Timothy. *The Reason for God: Belief in an Age of Skepticism*. New York: Riverhead Books, 2008.

Kuyper, Abraham. *Principles of Sacred Theology*. Grand Rapids: Eerdmans, 1963.

Lloyd-Jones, D. M. *Children of God*. Wheaton, IL: Crossway Books, 1993.

———. *Fellowship with God: Life in Christ: Volume one: Studies in 1 John*. Wheaton, IL: Crossway Books, 1993.

———. *Revival*. Wheaton. IL: Crossway, 1987.

———. *Walking with God*. Wheaton, IL: Crossway Books, 1993.

Bibliography

Lusk, Rich. "Do I Believe in Baptismal Regeneration?" Cited in Guy Prentiss Waters. *The Federal Vision and Covenant Theology: A Comparative Analysis*, 226–27. Phillipsburg, NJ: P&R Publishing, 2006.

Luther, Martin. "A Mighty Fortress Is Our God." In *Trinity Hymnal*, 92.

Mackintosh, Hugh Ross. *Types of Modern Theology*. New York: Scribner's Sons, n.d.

Martin, Hugh. *The Abiding Presence*. Edinburgh: Knox Press, n.d.

McLaren, Brian D. *A New Kind of Christian*. San Francisco: Jossey-Bass, 2008.

———. *A New Kind of Christianity: Ten Questions That Are Transforming the Faith*. New York: HarperOne, 2011.

McLean, B. H. *Biblical Interpretation and Philosophical Hermeneutics*. Cambridge: Cambridge University Press, 2012.

Murray, Iain. *Pentecost—Today?* Edinburgh: Banner of Truth, 1998.

Murray, John. *Collected Writings of John Murray: Volume one: The Claims of Truth*. Edinburgh: Banner of Truth, 1976.

———. *Redemption—Accomplished and Applied*. Grand Rapids: Eerdmans, 1955.

———. *The Epistle to the Romans*. Vol. 1. Grand Rapids: Eerdmans, 1959.

———. *The Imputation of Adam's Sin*. Grand Rapids: Eerdmans, 1959.

Newman, John Henry. "Praise to the Holiest in the height." In *Congregational Praise*, 71.

Nietzsche, Friedrich. "The Gay Science." In *The Portable Nietzsche*, 95. Edited and translated by Walter Kaufman. New York: Viking Penguin, 1982.

Oliphint, K. Scott. *Covenantal Apologetics*. Wheaton, IL: Crossway, 2013.

———. *God With Us: Divine Condescension and the Attributes of God*. Wheaton, IL: Crossway, 2102.

Owen, John. *The Death of Death in the Death of Christ*. Edinburgh: Banner of Truth, 1959.

———. "Of communion with God." In *The Works of John Owen*, 2:9–17. Edinburgh: Banner of Truth, 1966.

———. "The glory of Christ." In *The Works of John Owen*, 1:273–415. Edinburgh: Banner of Truth, 1965.

———. "The glory of Christ applied to sinners and saints." In *The Works of John Owen*, 1:417–61. Edinburgh: Banner of Truth, 1965.

———. "The Person of Christ." In *The Works of John Owen*, 1:1–271. Edinburgh: Banner of Truth, 1965.

———. *The Works of John Owen*. 16 vols. Edinburgh: Banner of Truth, 1965–68.

Packer, J. I. "Introductory Essay." In John Owen, *The Death of Death in the Death of Christ*, 1–25. Edinburgh: Banner of Truth, 1959.

Peterson, Robert A. *Calvin and the Atonement*. Fearn, Scotland: Christian Focus, Mentor imprint, 1999.

———. *Calvin's Doctrine of the Atonement*. Phillipsburg, NJ: Presbyterian and Reformed, 1983.

Poole, Matthew. *A Commentary on the Holy Bible, Volume III: Matthew–Revelation*. Edinburgh: Banner of Truth, 1963.

Pope, Alexander. "An Essay on Man." In M. H. Abrams, *The Norton Anthology of English Literature*, 770. New York: Norton, 1962.

Runes, Dagobert D. *Dictionary of Philosophy*. Ames: Littlefield, Adams, 1958.

Schaff, Philip. *The Creeds of Christendom*, 3 vols. Grand Rapids: Baker, 1996.

Schleiermacher, Friedrich. *The Christian Faith*. Edinburgh: T. & T. Clark, 1928.

Bibliography

Schweitzer, Albert. *The Quest for the Historical Jesus: A Critical Study of its Progress from Reimarus to Wrede*. Holmen, WI: Suzeteo Enterprises, 2011. Also available in various editions, including Kindle.

Shakespeare, William. *Sonnets to Sundry Notes of Music*, various editions.

Shedd, W. G. T. *A History of Christian Doctrine*. 2 vols. New York: Scribner's Sons, 1868.

———. *Dogmatic Theology*. 3 vols. Grand Rapids: Zondervan, n.d.

Shepherd, Norman. *The Call of Grace: How the Covenant Illuminates Salvation and Evangelism*. Phillipsburg, NJ: P&R Publishing, 2000.

Sprague, William B. *Lecures on Revivals of Religion*. Edinburgh: Banner of Truth, 1959.

Sproul, R. C. *Grace Unknown: The Heart of Reformed Theology*. Grand Rapids: Baker, 1997.

Strimple, Robert B. *The Modern Search for the Real Jesus*. Phillipsburg, NJ: P&R Publishing, 1995.

Tillich, Paul. *Systematic Theology: Volume 1: Reason and Revelation, Being, and God*. Chicago: University of Chicago Press, 1951.

Trinity Hymnal. Atlanta: Great Commission Publications, 1990.

Turretin, Francis. *Institutes of Elenctic Theology*. Translated by George Musgrave Giger. Edited by James T. Dennison, Jr. Vol 2. Phillipsburg, NJ: P&R Publishing, 1994.

Van Til, Cornelius. *A Christian Theory of Knowledge*. Philadelphia: Presbyterian and Reformed, 1969.

———. *An Introduction to Systematic Theology*. Philadelphia: Presbyterian and Reformed, 1974.

———. *The Defense of the Faith*. Philadelphia: Presbyterian and Reformed, 1955.

Venning, Ralph. *The Plague of Plagues*. Edinburgh: Banner of Truth, 1965.

Vickers, Douglas. *Being and Belief: A Plain View of the Christian Confession*. Eugene, OR: Wipf & Stock, 2103.

———. *Discovering the Christian Mind*. Eugene, OR: Wipf & Stock, 2011.

Warfield, B. B. *Biblical Doctrines*. Grand Rapids: Baker, 2003.

Waters, Guy Prentiss. *Justification and the New Perspective on Paul: A Review and Response*. Phillipsburg, NJ: P&R Publishing, 2004.

———. *The Federal Vision and Covenant Theology: A Comparative Analysis*. Phillipsburg, NJ: P&R Publishing, 2006.

Wesley, Charles. "Hark! The Herald Angels Sing." In *Trinity Hymnal*, 203.

Westminster Shorter Catechism. Various editions.

Windelband, W. *A History of Philosophy*. New York: Macmillan, 1921.

Wright, N. T. *What Saint Paul Really Said: Was Paul of Tarsus the Real Founder of Christianity?* Grand Rapids: Eerdmans, 1997.

Wright, R. K. McGregor. *No Place for Sovereignty: What's Wrong with Freewill Theism*. Downers Grove, IL: InterVarsity Press, 1996.

Young, Edward J. *My Servants the Prophets*. Grand Rapids: Eerdmans, 1952.